HE CHOSE YOU

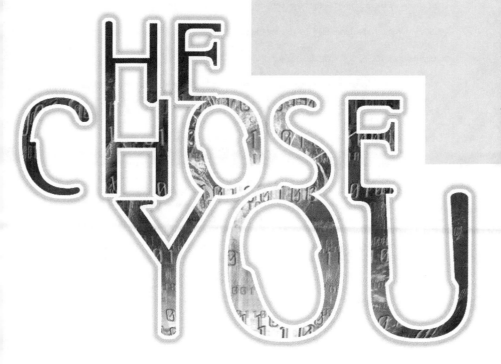

HE CHOSE YOU

adapted from HE CHOSE THE NAILS

lucado

with story adaptations by MONICA HALL

Published in Nashville, Tennessee, by Tommy Nelson®, a Division of Thomas Nelson, Inc.

Designed by Uttley/DouPonce DesignWorks, Sisters, Oregon.

Unless otherwise noted, Scripture quotations used in this book are from the Holy Bible, New Century Version® (NCV) copyright © 1987, 1988, 1991 by Word Publishing, Dallas, Texas 75234. Used by permission.

Other Scripture references are used by permission from the following sources:
The Contemporary English Version (CEV), copyright © 1995 by the American Bible Society. The International Children's Bible®, New Century Version® (ICB), copyright © 1986, 1989, 1999 by Tommy Nelson®, a Division of Thomas Nelson, Inc. The Message (MSG), copyright © 1993, 1994, 1995 by Eugene H. Peterson, NavPress Publishing Group. The New English Bible (NEB), copyright © 1961, 1970 by the delegates of the Oxford University Press and the Syndics of the Cambridge University Press in England. The Holy Bible, New International Version (NIV), copyright © 1973, 1978, 1984 by New York International Bible Society, Zondervan Bible Publishers. The King James Version of the Bible (KJV). The New King James Version (NKJV), copyright © 1979, 1980, 1982 by Thomas Nelson Inc. The Holy Bible, New Living Translation (NLT), copyright © 1996 by Tyndale House Publishers, Inc. The New Revised Standard Version Bible (NRSV), copyright © 1989 by the Division of Christian Education of the National Council of the Churches of Christ in the U.S.A. J. B. Phillips: The New Testament in Modern English, Revised Edition (PHILLIPS), copyright © J. B. Phillips 1958, 1960, 1972 by The Macmillian Company. The Good News Bible: Today's English Version (TEV), copyright © 1966, 1971, 1976 by the American Bible Society. The Living Bible (TLB), copyright © 1971 by Tyndale House Publishers.

Library of Congress Cataloging-in-Publication Data
Lucado, Max.
   He chose you / Max Lucado ; with story adaptations by Monica Hall.
     p. cm.
   Based on He chose the nails by Max Lucado.
   Summary: Combines passages from the author's book, "He Chose the Nails," with stories which explore Christ's love for human beings as evidenced in various aspects of his Crucifixion.
   ISBN 0-8499-7789-4
   1. Christian children--Religious life. 2. Christian teenagers--Religious life. 3. Jesus Christ--Person and offices--Juvenile literature. [1. Jesus Christ--Person and offices. 2. Christian life.] I. Hall, Monica. II. Title.

BV4571.3 .L83 2001
232--dc21   2001044850

Printed in the United States of America
02 03 04 05 06 PHX 5 4 3 2 1

To the Youth Program
of the Oak Hills Church of Christ—

Keep it up! You guys are awesome.

—M. L.

CONTENTS

ACKNOWLEDGMENTS

This book would not exist without the inspiration and hard work of several people.

Special thanks go to the Tommy Nelson team of Laura Minchew, Beverly Phillips, and June Ford.

Special appreciation to Monica Hall for writing the contemporary application stories interspersed in the chapters.

Karen Hill, my assistant and lifesaver, did a masterful job in editing and managing.

Three young friends graciously agreed to read the book and share their opinions: Chris Clark, Courtney Kunkel, and Salena Wiley.

Of course, the greatest credit goes to Jesus, without whom we'd have no story at all.

Dear Friend,

I'm so grateful that you are holding this book. Over the next few pages, you and I are going to explore the greatest event in history—the cross of Christ.

No event is more crucial. For if the events of the cross are true, then the cross is the solution to every problem of life. Forgiveness of sin, deliverance from death, purpose for life: All are found at the foot of the cross.

You are to be congratulated for taking time to ponder it. May God use these pages to bless you and show you the meaning of Calvary.

Max Lucado

Long ago, even before he made the world,
God loved us and chose us in Christ to be holy
and without fault in his eyes.
His unchanging plan has always been to adopt us into
his own family by bringing us to himself through Jesus Christ.
And this gave him great pleasure.
So we praise God for the wonderful kindness he has poured
out on us because we belong to his dearly loved Son.
He is so rich in kindness that he purchased our freedom
through the blood of his Son,
and our sins are forgiven . . .
God's secret plan has now been revealed to us;
it is a plan centered on Christ,
designed long ago according to his good pleasure.
And this is his plan:
At the right time he will bring everything together
under the authority of Christ—everything in heaven and on earth.
Furthermore, because of Christ,
we have received an inheritance from God,
for he chose us from the beginning,
and all things happen just as he decided long ago.

EPHESIANS 1:4–7, 9–11 NLT

1

Oh, the *Things* We Do for Love!

(God Did This for Me?!)

The gift of God is eternal life
in Christ Jesus our Lord.

ROMANS 6:23 NIV

Thanks be to God for his indescribable gift!

2 CORINTHIANS 9:15 NIV

Every good and perfect gift is from above,
coming down from the Father of the heavenly lights,
who does not change like shifting shadows.
He chose to give us birth through the word of truth,
that we might be a kind of firstfruits of all he created.

JAMES 1:17–18 NIV

One cautious knee at a time, Josh crept carefully forward, took a deep breath, and looked down over the edge. (Gulp!) It sure was a long . . . lonnnng . . . way to the ground from up here. And it had seemed like such a good idea at the time. (What *was* he thinking?!)

He closed his eyes for a moment—this was not a good time to get dizzy!—and settled back on his heels. Surely it wouldn't hurt to take just a small break before getting started—just long enough for his stomach to settle back into place. Besides, he reminded himself, it's for The Gift, so don't be such a wuss!

Josh couldn't exactly recall when it was he had the stroke of genius that brought him to this moment. But it was a good one—occasional moment of terror or not—he decided. After all, "creative solutions" were his specialty. And this was a doozy! Which is exactly what you need when you're too young for a real job and want to come up with a very special gift for a very special someone.

Just thinking about her made him smile. Being with her somehow always turned into an adventure—she found something to enjoy, or learn from, or celebrate in even the most ordinary things. And when she looked at him with those dazzling blue eyes and smiled at something he said or did, he felt ten feet tall. Because when she looked at him, she saw something . . . wonderful.

And she deserved a gift as special as she was. Whatever it took. Which is how he ended up on old Mrs. Carter's roof—looking at what must be miles of leaf-filled gutters!

Oh, the things we do to give gifts to those we love. We work hard, save our money, and shop carefully, or spend time thinking up and *making*—creative gifts for the special people in our lives.

But we don't mind, do we? We would do it all again. Fact is, we *do* it all again. Every Christmas, every birthday—every so often—we find ourselves in foreign territory. On purpose. A choice made of our own free will. Grownups are in toy stores. Dads are in teen stores. Wives are in the fishing department, and husbands are in the purse department.

Not only do we enter unusual places, we do unusual things. We mow lawns to buy Dad that special tool or baby-sit in order to buy Mom her favorite perfume.

And we'd do it all again. Having pressed the grapes of service, we drink life's sweetest wine—the wine of giving. We are at our best when we are giving. In fact, we are most like God when we are giving.

There! Josh scooped up the last handful of slimy, mushy—yucky!—leaves from the gutter and dropped them to the ground. Finally done. Now all he had to do was rake up the mess on the grass and his Mrs. Carter projects were finished. Of course, *first* he had to get off the roof, down the ladder, and back on good old solid ground. High places were definitely *not* his thing. But he had to admit, the view from up here was great.

He gave the gutter a good-bye pat and took a last look around—admiring the flower beds he'd cleaned out last weekend and the gleaming coat of fresh paint on that shabby old fence. Then he picked up his T-shirt (where *did* that big rip come from?!) and slipped it on. Ouch! *Oh well, a little sunburn never hurt anyone. And The Gift was worth it!*

The ladder started to slide...

Rung by careful rung, he started down the ladder—

"Yoo-hoo, Josh . . . I brought you some lemonade, dear."

Josh jumped. The ladder started to slide . . .

"Oh, my, are you all right, dear?" Mrs. Carter bent down to brush at his shirt (*and* sunburn) with tiny, frail hands.

"Uh . . . I think so," he answered, looking up at her. Then he cautiously tested each arm and leg. Everything seemed to work. Fortunately. *Wow, got lucky that time. One more trip to the emergency room and Mom would really freak out!*

"See, I'm fine. Really. Happens all the time," he said, bouncing to his feet and taking a few steps. (The limp hardly showed at all.)

"Well, if you're sure, dear . . ." Mrs. Carter still looked a little worried, but she managed a beaming smile when he posed her in front of her freshly painted fence, handed her the sign, and snapped the photo.

If she only knew! Josh grinned to himself as he thought of *some* of the close calls he'd had in pursuit of The Gift.

Bathing and grooming the Andersons' five dogs, for instance. Funny, they hadn't looked quite so . . . big—or hairy—when he took on the job. And who would have guessed that sleepy old Bruno would make such a big deal about those snarls in his coat? (*Should have named* him *Fang!*) But it made a great photo. So did the big grins on those kids at the new playground he'd helped with—learning a thing or two about hammers in the process.

All in all, he'd managed to survive the last three months more or less intact, in spite of what his parents had thought when he came up with the idea for The Gift. In fact, they loved the idea itself.

"It's perfect," said his dad.

"Exactly what she'd like better than anything else," agreed Mom.

"But . . . ," cautioned Dad, "absolutely no sharp edges or power tools!" Dad still hadn't gotten over that little lawn mower fiasco. "You know what happens . . ."

Had to admit, Dad had a point. And Josh *was* on a first-name basis with every ER doctor in five counties. It wasn't that he was careless. Things just seemed to . . . happen. If something was going to fall, chances were really good it would fall on Josh. Sharp, pointy objects could find him in the dark. Doorways were never quite wide enough. Curbs, foot-stools—even the dog dish!—threw themselves in his path. And every bee or wasp with an attitude had his address.

So power tools were out. But there were plenty of *other* odd jobs that needed doing. And people—like Mrs. Carter—who really couldn't afford to hire a professional to do them. And when they heard about The Gift—and saw how hard he worked to make every job a *perfect* job—he had all the work he could handle. And more.

A few scrapes, bruises, and "dings" were a small price to pay for what he had in mind. And, hey, a sprained ankle could happen to anyone. Though that problem with the wallpaper paste *was* kind of a surprise. But he'd needed a haircut anyway . . .

Have you ever wondered why God gives so much? We could exist on far less. He could have left the world flat and gray; we wouldn't have known the difference. But he didn't.

> *He splashed orange in the sunrise*
> *and cast the sky in blue.*
> *And if you love to see geese as they gather,*
> *chances are you'll see that too.*

Did he have to make the squirrel's tail furry?

Was he obliged to make the birds sing?

And the funny way that chickens scurry

or the majesty of thunder when it rings?

Why give a flower fragrance? Why give food its taste?

Could it be

he loves to see

that look upon your face?

If we give gifts to show our love, how much more would he? If we—speckled with quirks and greed—love to give gifts, how much more does God, pure and perfect God, enjoy giving gifts to us? Jesus asked, "If you hardhearted, sinful men know how to give good gifts to your children, won't your Father in heaven even more certainly give good gifts to those who ask him for them?" (Matthew 7:11 TLB).

Every gift reveals God's love...

Gifts shed light on God's heart, God's good and generous heart. Jesus' brother James tells us: "Every desirable and beneficial gift comes out of heaven. The gifts are rivers of light cascading down from the Father of Light" (James 1:17 MSG). Every gift reveals God's love ... but no gift reveals his love more than the gifts of the cross. They came, not wrapped in paper, but in passion. Not placed around a tree, but a cross. And not covered with ribbons, but sprinkled with blood. The gifts of the cross.

Much has been said about the gift of the cross itself, but what of the other gifts? What of the nails, the crown of thorns? The garments taken by the soldiers. The garments given for the burial. Have you taken time to open these gifts? To see them for what they are? To think about what they *mean?* Do you understand the incredible love wrapped *inside* each gift?

Josh scooted around very carefully on the rickety folding chair. *Please, no disasters today!* He glanced down at The Gift, then looked around the crowded athletic field and tried not to yawn as the speeches went on and on. *Bor-ing!*

Finally—an eternity or two later—they were ready to hand out the diplomas. Josh searched the long line of caps and gowns with eager eyes—looking for *her.* There! Smack-dab in the middle of the parade of solemn twenty-somethings—practically bouncing with excitement—there she was. Flashing blue eyes. Enormous grin. And a riot of shining silver curls. Gran—*his* Gran was graduating from college!

Gran: who had filled Josh's life with love and joy, and taught him that every day was a gift—and a chance to do "just a little good, Josh, just a little . . ."

Gran: who not only approved of the Golden Rule, but was convinced it was her personal responsibility to make it shine.

Gran: who saw service to others as a privilege, and positively knew that anyone who needed a helping hand was her neighbor!

Gran: who believed in dreams, and in making them come true.

After ten long years of day jobs and night classes, Gran was graduating from college! And Josh was about to burst with love and pride.

"Here, Gran," said Josh with a big hug, "this is for you."

Gran looked puzzled as she began leafing through the photo album. But then she took a closer look and began to smile.

Page by page, photo by photo, her smile grew bigger as she studied the beaming faces. Mrs. Carter and her freshly painted fence. Five extremely well-groomed dogs sitting politely beside Tom Anderson's wheelchair. The Head Start kids on their new playground. Josh himself surrounded by twenty bags of trash collected in that eyesore vacant lot. The freshly washed windows at the homeless shelter . . .

Page by page the story unfolded. And in every photo of every "gift" a grinning someone was holding a big sign that read: **For Gran . . . with Love!**

"Oh, Josh . . . this must have taken months!" Gran's voice shook just the tiniest bit.

Josh gave her another hug. "Well, of course, Gran. That was the whole idea. Besides, there were a lot of people who needed a hand."

"I . . . I've never had such a lovely gift. I don't know what to say," said Gran, who usually *did*.

"Oh, you already said it, Gran," he answered, "lots of times. Remember? 'The best gifts are the ones that come from the heart, with a little bit of the giver inside.'"

"And believe me, Gran," chimed in Dad, with a pointed glance at the bandage on Josh's forehead and the cast on his wrist, "there are *several* bits of Josh in this gift!"

Which was okay, since everyone needed a laugh right about then.

Jesus didn't have to give us so *many* gifts at the cross, you know. The only act, the only *required* act for our salvation was the shedding of blood, yet he did much more. So much more. Search the scene of the cross, and what do you find?

A wine-soaked sponge.

A sign.

Two crosses beside Christ.

Gifts, each and every one. Divine gifts intended to stir that moment, that split second when your face will brighten, your eyes will widen, and God will hear you whisper, "You did this for me?"

The diadem of pain
which sliced your gentle face,
three spikes piercing flesh and wood
to hold you in your place.

The need for blood I understand.
Your sacrifice I embrace.
But the bitter sponge, the cutting spear,
the spit upon your face?
Did it have to be a cross?
Did not a kinder death exist
than six hours hanging between life and death,
all spurred by a betrayer's kiss?

"Oh, Father," you pose,
heart-stilled at what could be,
"I'm sorry to ask, but I long to know,
did you do this for me?"

Dare we pray such a prayer? Dare we think such thoughts? Could it be that the hill of the cross is rich with God's gifts? Let's examine them, shall we? Let's unwrap these gifts of grace as if—or perhaps, indeed—for the first time. And as you touch them—as you feel the timber of the cross and trace the braid of the crown and finger the point of the spike—pause and listen. Perhaps you'll hear him whisper . . .

"I did it just for you."

2

Spit, Sin, and Other Nasty Stuff We'd Rather Not Think About

"I Will Bear Your Dark Side"
(God's Promise in the Soldiers' Spit)

Sin speaks to the wicked man in his heart.

PSALM 36:1 ICB

Foolish people don't care if they sin.
But honest people work at being right with others.

PROVERBS 14:9 ICB

So, do not let sin control you in your life
here on earth. You must not be ruled by the things
your sinful self makes you want to do.

ROMANS 6:12 ICB

Spit?! Eeuwwww! Pretty nasty stuff, right? Not that you'd ever do anything that ugly, of course. Jenny Archer certainly wouldn't.

Or so she thought.

But we'll get to that in a minute. First, let me ask you something: Have you ever wondered what would have happened to the Beast if the Beauty hadn't come along?

You know the story. There was a time when his face was handsome and his palace pleasant. But that was before the curse. Before the shadows fell on the castle of the prince. Before the shadows fell on the heart of the prince. And when the shadows fell, he hid. Locked away in his castle, he was left with a glistening snout and curly tusks . . . and in a very bad mood.

All that changed, of course, when the girl came. But what if she hadn't appeared?

Even worse, what would have happened if she hadn't *cared?* And who would have blamed her if she hadn't? He was such a . . . well, such a beast. Hairy. Drooling. Roaring. Angry! And she was such a beauty. Stunningly gorgeous. Contagiously kind. If ever two people lived up to their names, didn't the Beauty and the Beast? Who would have blamed her if she hadn't cared?

But she did care.

And because the Beauty loved the Beast, the Beast became more beautiful himself.

Just a fairy tale, right? That's why the story feels so familiar. Sure, that's part of it. But do you know another reason why this story feels so familiar? Because it reminds us of ourselves. Because—and here's the really scary part—there's a beast inside each of us!

It wasn't always so. There was a time when the face of humanity was beautiful and the palace pleasant. But that was before the curse. Before the shadow fell across the garden of Adam. Before the shadow fell across the heart of Adam. And ever since the curse we've been different. Beastly. Ugly. Defiant. Angry!

We do things—unkind, hateful things—we know we shouldn't. Then we wonder why we did them.

Jenny's beast woke and stretched and bared its teeth in—of all places—the Jefferson Middle School cafeteria, on a sunny October Monday.

Jenny looked doubtfully at the steaming pan of . . . something. *Oh, please,* she thought, watching a dripping ladle scoop out a hearty portion, *not Mystery Meat again!*

But before she could shake her head no . . . *Splat!* Lunch (or whatever it was) landed with a splashy plop onto her tray—and onto the front of her new shirt. (First her stubborn hair, then math, now *this!*)

"Well, of course," she sighed, "it's *that* kind of day!" Then she jumped as the next tray in line slammed into hers, pinching her fingers between the two.

"Oh, sorry, Jen," said a cheerful voice.

"Well, really, Brian!" huffed Jenny.

"You okay?" asked Brian, not used to seeing sunny, "together" Jenny looking so . . . frazzled.

"Oh, you know"—she shrugged as they headed for the table the "crew" always shared—"it's just one of those Mondays."

"Know what ya mean." He grinned.

"Hey, guys," said Jenny, sliding into her seat beside Emma. She managed a weak smile across the table at Karen, Lisa, Annie, and Zack. She felt better already, just being with these friends she'd had practically *forever*. So what if her morning had been mega-grim? The afternoon would go just fine, she decided. (And things usually did go the way Jenny wanted them to go.)

"How was math today, Jen? Any better?" asked Emma in a most motherly voice. She knew how hard Jenny was struggling in that class—and how much she hated not being the best at whatever she did.

"Please, Em," Jenny groaned with a dramatic roll of tragic green eyes, "don't ask." Then she grinned. "At least not until I get my brain into gear."

And I will! she promised herself silently. *If that weirdo new girl can sail through it, so can I!*

"Oh, my, look at that," breathed Lisa, not at all interested in math. "Who is that? And where *did* she get those clothes?!"

Six heads turned to see what had caught Lisa's attention this time. There! Over by the wall stood a tall girl with tightly cropped hair and a pale angular face balancing books, a backpack, and lunch tray.

"Wow," offered Zack.

Which pretty much summed it up. In a room full of khakis and pastels, she was a vision in . . . black. Black! Every stitch. Every fiber. Every garment. Black—from her ragged cap of midnight hair to the scuffed toes of her heavy boots.

Annie giggled. "Oh dear, wait till the Dress Code Police see that!"

"And did you ever see so many earrings?!" chimed in Karen, somewhere between disapproval and awe.

"Probably pulls in satellite **TV** *without* a dish," Zack teased.

"She looks lonely," said Emma softly. "I wonder who she is."

"Her name is Jez. She's from Chicago, where *everyone* is way cooler—and smarter—than we are here in the 'Boonies'!" came Jenny's tart reply.

Emma looked at her friend, surprised. Jenny was usually the first with a friendly smile, the one who led the way in making people feel welcome. Who was this stranger sitting next to her? And what had she done with the *real* Jen?!

It surprised Jenny, too. *Why did I say that?* she wondered. (Although, to be honest, she knew exactly why.)

Like the apostle Paul, Jenny had just run headlong into one of life's biggest struggles. "I do not understand the things I do. I do not do the good things I want to do. And I do the bad things I hate to do" (Romans 7:15 ICB).

Ever feel like that?

If so, you're in good company. Paul isn't the only person in the Bible who wrestled the beast within. In fact, it's hard to find a page in Scripture where the animal doesn't bare his teeth: King Saul chasing young David with a spear, the sons of Jacob murdering Shechem and his friends, Lot tempted by the wickedness of Sodom, Herod murdering Bethlehem toddlers.

"...I do the bad things I hate to do."

If the Bible is called the Good Book, it's not because its people always are. But the evil of the beast was never so terrible as on the day Jesus died.

His disciples—his friends!—were fast asleep when he needed them most and then ran fast away when things got tough.

Herod wanted a show.

Pilate just wanted it all to go away.

And the soldiers? They wanted blood.

So they scourged Jesus—with a cruel whip made of leather straps with a tiny lead ball on the end of each. The idea was simple: Beat the prisoner almost—but not quite—to death, and then stop. Thirty-nine lashes were allowed, but seldom needed. An officer kept careful watch to make sure the prisoner wasn't accidentally killed—before he could be properly executed! Jesus was probably very near death when his hands were untied and he slumped to the ground.

The whipping was the first deed of the soldiers.

The crucifixion was the third. (No, I didn't skip the second. We'll get to that in a moment.) Though his back was ribboned with wounds, the soldiers loaded the crossbeam onto his shoulders and marched him to the Place of a Skull and executed him.

Cruel as those two actions were, the soldiers were, after all, just following their orders. But what's so hard to understand is the terrible thing they did in between. Here's what Matthew tells us:

> Pilate told some of the soldiers to beat Jesus with whips. Then he gave Jesus to the soldiers to be killed on a cross.

> Pilate's soldiers took Jesus into the governor's palace. All the soldiers gathered around Jesus. They took off his clothes and put a red robe on him. Then the soldiers used thorny branches to make a crown. They put this crown of thorns on Jesus' head. They put a stick in his right hand. Then the soldiers bowed before Jesus and made fun of him. They said, "Hail, King of the Jews!" *They spit on Jesus.* Then they took his stick and hit him on the head many times. After they finished making fun of Jesus, the soldiers took off the robe and put his own clothes on him again. Then they led Jesus away to be killed on a cross. (Matthew 27:26–31 ICB, italics mine)

The soldiers' assignment was simple: Take Jesus to the hill and kill him. But they had another idea. They wanted to have some fun first. Strong, rested, armed soldiers surrounded an exhausted, nearly dead carpenter—and beat up on him.

The scourging was commanded. The crucifixion was ordered. But why on earth would anyone take pleasure in spitting on a half-dead man?

Spitting isn't intended to hurt the body. It can't. Spitting is meant to wound the soul, to make someone feel small and worthless. And it does.

What were the soldiers doing? Ah, you know, don't you? They were raising themselves up by putting someone else down. They were making themselves feel big by making Jesus look small.

"What?" asked Jenny, very busy with a stray lock of her copper-colored hair, trying to act as if nothing unusual had just happened. *Why is Emma looking so shocked, anyway?* she thought. *Who said I had to like every new kid in school?*

"Well . . . ," said Emma cautiously, "she just looked so alone. And it's got to be hard to be new *and* so . . . different. I guess you know her?"

Jenny shrugged. "Everyone in math class knows her!" *How could we miss her?* she thought. *Sitting on the edge of her seat like that. Nodding and smiling before Mrs. Allen was even halfway through explaining. Acting like it was all so easy!*

21

"Well, she seems to know *you*," Karen whispered.

Sure enough, in that busy, crowded lunchroom, those cool gray eyes had somehow found Jenny's table—Jenny . . . and the empty chair beside her. (Sometimes having hair the exact color of a new penny was *not* a blessing!)

"How 'bout it, Jen? Want to ask her over?" That was Zack—who could never resist anything new.

"There's room," pointed out Emma.

It was up to Jenny. All she had to do was lift her hand and wave. A stranger would be made welcome. Jez could start off in her new school knowing some pretty neat kids. Jenny might even get a little help with math.

All she had to do was wave. Jenny knew it. Her friends knew it. Jez knew it—though you'd never have guessed from the proud tilt of her chin that it made the slightest bit of difference what happened. All she did was look at Jenny—gray eyes meeting green—and wait.

Jenny knew what she *should* do. She also knew what she *wanted* to do. Slowly, her hand lifted. Hesitated. Then reached down, picked up her backpack . . . and set it firmly onto the empty chair beside her.

"Trust me, guys," she said, "she's just not our kind."

Ever done anything like that? Maybe you've never actually spit on anyone, as the soldiers did. But then neither did Jenny—exactly. But there's spit ... and spit. Have you ever gossiped? Rolled your eyes to make someone feel dumb? Blasted a friend with angry words? Made someone feel bad so you could feel good?

That's what the soldiers did to Jesus. And when you and I do the same to someone else, we do it to Jesus, too. "I assure you, when you did it to one of the least of these my brothers and sisters, you were doing it to me!" (Matthew 25:40 NLT).

How we treat others is how we treat Jesus.

I don't like to hear that, you're thinking. Believe me, I don't like to say it. But the fact is, there is something beastly inside each and every one of us. Something beastly that makes us do things that surprise us. Haven't you surprised yourself like that? Thought about something you've done and wondered, *What got into me?*

The Bible has a three-letter answer for that question: S-I-N. That's what got into you. And me. And every human since Adam's fall. Sin— beastly and bad—lurks within each of us. Sharpening its teeth. Waiting.

It's not that we *can't* do good. We can—and do. It's just that we can't always keep from doing bad things. Sometimes, it comes out when we least expect it. That's what happened to Jenny, who would usually just laugh off a "bad day." But this time, Jenny—who liked being the best, who just couldn't stand it when the math that was so hard for her was so easy for Jez—made sure Jez felt just as bad as she did.

Although we were made in God's image, we have fallen. David said, "I was brought into this world in sin" (Psalm 51:5 ICB). Can any of us say any less? The fact is, each of us was born with a tendency to sin. Scripture says it plainly:

We all have wandered away like sheep. Each of us has gone his own way. (Isaiah 53:6 ICB)

The heart is deceitful above all things and beyond cure. Who can understand it? (Jeremiah 17:9 NIV)

There is no one without sin. None! . . . All people have sinned and are not good enough for God's glory. (Romans 3:10, 23 ICB)

Pretty strong words, right? Maybe *too* strong? Some people might look around and say, "Compared to everyone else, I'm a pretty decent person." The thing is, a pig could say the same thing. He could look around at his trough partners and decide, "I'm just as clean as everyone else!" Compared to humans, however, that pig needs help! Compared to God, we humans need the same. The standard for sinlessness isn't found at the pig troughs of earth, but at the throne of heaven. God himself is the standard.

We don't like what we do. And— by ourselves— we can't change!

That's the bad news: We carry darkness—sin—inside ourselves. Here's the even worse news: We're stuck with it! Our deeds are ugly. Our actions are harsh. We don't do what we want to. We don't like what we do. And—by ourselves—we can't change!

We try; oh, how we try. But "a leopard cannot change his spots. In the same way, Jerusalem, you cannot change and do good. You always do evil" (Jeremiah 13:23 ICB). The apostle agreed with the prophet: "If a person's thinking is controlled by his sinful self, then he is against God. He refuses to obey God's law. And really he is not able to obey God's law" (Romans 8:7 ICB).

No! you may be thinking, *that can't be right.* Are you sure? Really? Then try this: For the next twenty-four hours, lead a sinless life. I'm not asking for a perfect year or even a perfect month. Just one perfect day. Can you do it? Can you live without sin for one day?

No? How about one hour? Could you promise that for the next sixty minutes you will have only good thoughts and actions?

Not so sure? Then how about the next five minutes? Just five minutes of loving, anger-free, unselfish living—can you do it?

No? Neither can I.

So we have a problem: We are sinners, and "the wages of sin is death" (Romans 6:23 NIV).

We have a problem: We are not holy, and "if anyone's life is not holy, he will never see the Lord" (Hebrews 12:14 ICB).

We have a problem: We are evil, and "evil people are paid back with punishment" (Proverbs 10:16 ICB).

What can we do? By ourselves, nothing.

What can Jesus do? Everything.

And he did it when he took the darkness in our hearts—as he did the soldiers' spit on his face—and carried it to the cross. And there, mixed in with his sweat and blood, he wore the slimy filth of every sin ever committed.

God could have arranged things differently. In God's plan, Jesus was offered wine for his throat, so why not a towel for his face? Simon carried the cross of Jesus, but he didn't wipe the cheek of Jesus. Angels were just a prayer away. Couldn't they have taken the spit away?

They could have, but Jesus never commanded them to. For some reason, the One who chose the nails also chose the spit. Along with the whip and thorns of man, he bore the spit of man. Why? Could it be that he sees the beauty within the beast?

But here we move beyond the fairy tale, to something much more wondrous. In the fable, the beauty kisses the beast. In the Bible, the Beauty does much more. He *becomes* the Beast, so the beast can become the beauty. Jesus changes places with us! Like Adam, we were under a curse, but Jesus "changed places with us and put himself under that curse" (Galatians 3:13 ICB). The sinless One took on the face of a sinner, so that we sinners could take on the face of love.

What if the Beauty had not come? What if the Beauty had not *cared?* Then we would have remained a beast.

But the Beauty did come, and the Beauty did care.

Concentrate, Jen. Concentrate! *Stroke. Stroke. Stroke. Breathe. Stroke. Stroke. Breathe . . . Drat!* Arms flying, feet kicking, Jenny coughed and spit out a mouthful of pool water.

Swim team practice was not going well. Try as she would, she just couldn't seem to slice through the water with her usual quick grace. Something seemed to be holding her back. (A guilty conscience can be a real drag, you know.)

She should have been focused on the finish line. But what she saw instead was the look on Jez's face today—in the cafeteria, when she'd snubbed her.

Stop it! she told herself. *That was then, this is now. And now is swimming!* Which still wasn't going well at all. In fact, someone was passing her in the next lane! That *never* happened!

Jenny dug in and found a burst of speed. But it wasn't enough. Another hand touched the wall first, then pulled a slender body up onto the deck.

Out of breath, Jenny stared up at the tall girl in the black swimsuit. She felt something stir inside—something nasty. *Down!* she told it silently. Then she laughed. "Good grief, Jez, *please* tell me you're not a math whiz *and* champion swimmer."

Jez studied her thoughtfully for a long moment. Then she grinned. "Naaah, this was just luck." She reached out a hand to pull Jenny up beside her. "Now the math thing, though . . ."

Jenny grinned back. "To tell the truth, I could use a hand with that, too. Want to talk about it tomorrow? At lunch?"

Jenny dug in and found a burst of speed. But it wasn't enough.

The Ultimate "Been There, Done That!"

"I Loved You Enough to Become One of You"
(God's Promise in the Crown of Thorns)

God was pleased for all of himself to live in Christ.
Colossians 1:19 icb

The Word became a man and lived among us.
We saw his glory—the glory that belongs
to the only Son of the Father.
The Word was full of grace and truth.
John 1:14 icb

The Father and I are one.
John 10:30 icb

Have you ever looked at someone you liked—or admired—and wondered what it would be like to *be* that person? How it would feel to be that smart . . . talented . . . popular . . . whatever? Walk around in their skin? Find out what makes them tick? Sounds pretty cool, right?

But what if it was someone you *didn't* admire? Someone who annoyed, puzzled, scared, or frustrated you? Someone who did strange or ugly things for no good reason you could see? Maybe not quite so cool.

Have you ever wondered what it would be like to walk in someone else's shoes?

If you asked Brian Parnell that question, what came back would probably be one of his famous "you're kidding, right?" looks. Because Brian had shoes of his own—special shoes—and they suited him just fine, thankyouverymuch!

The *slap, slap, slap* of Brian's track shoes beat out the rhythm of a music only *he* could hear. It had always been that way. When he ran—and he couldn't remember a time when he hadn't run—it was to the beat of a silent song playing inside his head.

Faster! called the music. *Faster!* And faster he went.

Fly . . . coaxed the song. And fly he did.

Brian was *born* to run, everyone said. "Not so," corrected his mother with a grin. "Brian was born *running.* In fact . . . ," she said as the grin got a little bigger, "Brian wasn't so much born as *launched* from some celestial starting blocks . . . and he hasn't stopped since!"

Which was pretty much true. If there was a race to run, Brian was in it . . . usually in the lead. Waaaay in the lead. 220. 440. The mile. All the same to "Brian the Bold" (which was his dad's name for the lean, agile son who'd skipped crawling and toddling entirely, to charge into life at a dead run). The music called, and Brian ran. Simple as that.

Usually. But not today. Today—on a cross-country training run for Friday's meet—the beat was a little . . . off. The music slightly out of tune. Because Brian had brought along his secret—his horrible little secret—on *this* run.

Brian liked to think of himself as a pretty nice guy. And most of the other kids would agree. People just naturally liked Brian, and he liked them right back. He went out of his way to be friendly and thoughtful, and "real." And the legendary "Brian smile" could light up a room.

Except . . . *except* when he was around people with disabilities. No matter how hard he tried—and he tried *very* hard (which might have been the problem)—he just couldn't get his act together with them. His voice got a little too loud (*as if they were deaf, too, for heaven's sake!*). And his smile got a little too big (*and phony!*).

Which bothered him a lot, because Brian really *was* a nice guy. But the truth was, people like Mark—who was in a wheelchair—just made him . . . uncomfortable. He didn't know why, any more than he knew why Mark was *in* the wheelchair. (The grapevine said he'd suffered a broken spine when he was in an accident a few years ago.)

In fact, that wheelchair seemed to bother Brian a lot more than it did Mark—who just got on with things. Zipping around the halls. Making friends. Carving out a place for himself . . . with everyone but Brian, that is. Brian usually managed to be somewhere else whenever Mark was around. And today . . . *today*, he'd actually looked away, pretending not to see Mark's friendly wave—

Give it a rest! Mark probably thought you just didn't see him. Find the music . . . find the music!

With an impatient shake of his head, he picked up the pace. Head up, arms pumping, Brian—and his secret—flew down the dirt road.

He never saw the pothole at all. . . .

You know the coolest thing about the coming of Christ? You know the most remarkable part of the incarnation?

Not just that he swapped eternity for calendars. Though such an exchange deserves our notice.

Scripture says that the number of God's years is unsearchable (Job 36:26). We may search out the moment the first wave slapped on a shore or the first star burst in the sky, but we'll never find the first moment when God was God, for there is no moment when God was not God. He has never *not been*, for he is eternal. God is not bound by time.

But when Jesus came to the earth, all this changed. He heard for the first time a phrase never used in heaven: "Your time is up." As a child, he had to leave the Temple because his time was up. As a man, he had to leave Nazareth because his time was up. And as a Savior, he had to die because his time was up. For thirty-three years, the stallion of heaven lived in the corral of time.

That's certainly remarkable, but there is something even *more* so. You want to see the brightest jewel in the treasure of Jesus' incarnation? You might think it was the fact that he lived in a body. One moment he was a boundless spirit; the next he was flesh and bones. Just like us. Remember the words of King David? "Where can I go to get away from your Spirit? Where can I run from you? If I go up to the heavens, you are there. If I lie down in the grave, you are there. If I rise with the sun in the east and settle in the west beyond the sea, even there you would guide me" (Psalm 139:7–10).

Our asking "Where is God?" is like a fish asking "Where is water?" or a bird asking "Where is air?" God is everywhere! Equally present in Cairo or Chicago. As active in the lives of Icelanders as in the lives of

> Our asking "Where is God?" is like a fish asking "Where is water?"

Texans. The dominion of God is "from sea to sea and from the River to the ends of the earth" (Psalm 72:8 NIV). We cannot *find* a place where God is not.

Yet when God entered time and became a man, he who was boundless became bound. Imprisoned in flesh. Restricted by weary-prone muscles and eyelids. For more than thirty years, his once limit-less reach would be limited to the stretch of an arm, his measureless speed checked to the pace of human feet.

It was a bad break, the doctor said.

Wrong! thought Brian, glaring down at the cast on his leg. *It was a lousy break! The absolute . . . pits!*

No Friday meet. No Regionals. No State Championships. Brian the Bold, Brian the Fleet, Brian the *Runner* was out for the season! And that wasn't even the worst part.

What hurt most of all—if you didn't count the ache of a healing bone—was being trapped in a body that didn't *work* the way he expected it to work. Instead of running, he hob-bled. Instead of leaping up from his desk, he practically had to pry himself out of his seat. As for weaving smoothly through the crowded halls between bells? Well, just try *that* on crutches. Why *had* they made the hallways so narrow any-way? And stairs? Don't ask!

"Hey, Brian, how's it going, man?"

"Pretty good, Zack, pretty good." Which was the answer he usually gave, no matter who asked, or how he really felt.

After all, there was no point in dumping on your friends. They'd been great. Lots of cards and calls while he was in the hospital. And some of the things they'd written on his cast—especially Jenny's little verse—were hilarious. And now that he was back in school they all tried really hard—maybe *too* hard—to pretend nothing had changed.

But it had, of course. They saved him a seat at lunch, but probably were getting pretty tired of tripping over his crutches. They included him in all their plans, but he could *feel* them waiting for him to catch up a lot of the time. Lisa just gave him a forgiving smile when he snapped at her for picking up the books he'd dropped. (And Lisa was *not* the forgiving type!) And no one—no one—ever mentioned track or used the word *run*.

The truth was, Brian was working up a really good case of self-pity—until he called a halt to that whole "poor me" business.

Cool it, Brian! It's not like you'll be this way forever, he reminded himself. *There are a lot of people who have it a lot worse. A lot worse!*

The truth was, all of this had come as a big surprise to Brian, who usually took things pretty much in stride. So he had to be in a cast for a month or two, what could be so hard about that?! What he hadn't expected was the daily "grind" of the whole thing. What a drag it was—even heavier than the cast itself—for a fleet-footed racer to be slow, awkward, and . . . earthbound!

Most of all, he was just plain fed up with feeling so "different," and making his friends feel so . . . uncomfortable.

What he wouldn't give—just for a moment—to feel that powerful surge of energy, that smooth flex of obedient muscles once again. To fly down the track. Drink the wind. Follow the music.

Do you suppose Jesus ever felt cramped in his human body? Tempted to reclaim his boundlessness—if only for a moment? In the middle of a long trip on aching feet, did he ever consider transporting himself to the next city? When the rain chilled his bones, was he tempted to change the weather? When the heat parched his lips, did he ever give thought to popping over to the Caribbean for some refreshment?

If he ever entertained such thoughts, he never gave in to them. Not once. Stop and think about this. Not once did Christ use his supernatural powers for personal comfort. With one word he could've transformed the hard earth into a soft bed, but he didn't. With a wave of his hand, he could've boomeranged the spit of his accusers back into their faces, but he didn't. With an arch of his brow, he could've paralyzed the hand of the soldier as he braided the crown of thorns. But he didn't.

Remarkable. But is this the *most* remarkable part of Jesus' coming? Many would argue not. Many, perhaps most, people would

A crown of thorns. A crown of... consequences.

point beyond his surrender of timelessness and boundlessness to his surrender of *sinlessness!* It's easy to see why.

Isn't this the message of the crown of thorns?

An unnamed soldier took branches—mature enough to bear thorns, nimble enough to bend—and wove them into a crown of mockery. A crown of thorns. A crown of . . . *consequences.*

Consequences?! Oh, yes. Just take a look anywhere in Scripture and you'll see that what thorns symbolize is not sin itself, but the *results* of sin. Remember Eden? After Adam and Eve sinned, God cursed the land: "So I will put a curse on the ground . . . The ground will produce thorns and weeds for you, and you will eat the plants of the field" (Genesis 3:17–18). Brambles on the earth are the product of sin in the heart.

Rebellion against God results in thorns: "Evil people's lives are like paths covered with thorns and traps" (Proverbs 22:5). Jesus even compared the lives of evil people to a thornbush. In speaking of false prophets, he said, "You will know these people by what they do. Grapes don't come from thornbushes, and figs don't come from thorny weeds" (Matthew 7:16).

The result of sin is thorns, Scripture tells us—spiny, prickly, cutting thorns. And in the thorny crown on Jesus' brow, don't we see a picture of the pain our sins cause him?

Step into the brier patch of humanity and feel a few sharp

reminders. Shame. Fear. Disgrace. Discouragement. Worry. Haven't our hearts—hasn't *your* heart—felt their sting?

The heart of Jesus, however, had not. He had never felt any of those things. He had never been cut by the thorns of sin. What you and I face every day, he never knew. Worry? He never felt anxious! Guilt? He was never guilty! Fear? He never left the presence of God! Jesus never knew the fruits of sin . . . until he *became* sin for us. Until he became one of us.

For Brian, the last straw—or maybe it was the *first*, depending on how you looked at it—came when he was almost out of the woods. One more week, and the cast was coming off!

Hang in there, Brian. Hang in there. Not much longer now. Which was good advice, he thought wryly, but not at all helpful at this particular moment. Swaying on his crutches. Trying to shift and balance backpack, books, *and* duffel. In front of these big, heavy—very *closed*—double doors to the courtyard.

Okay, try this: lunch bag in the teeth, duffel in your left hand. Open the door with your right. Wait a minute! That doesn't leave any hand for your crutches . . .

Of course, he had only himself to blame. Emma had offered to carry those extra books. And Josh would have been glad to walk along with him and get the door. But he was *tired* of having people do things for him. Like he was totally helpless—*and* . . . useless!

"Need a hand?" A swish of rubber tires, and a sleek, racy wheelchair swooped past Brian. With a practiced move, a grinning Mark spun his chair around with one hand, reached out with the other, and pulled the door open. "Be my guest."

And the light dawned.

It wasn't Mark who made him uncomfortable. It wasn't even the wheelchair that made him uncomfortable. It was worry that he might say or do something that would remind Mark that he couldn't walk or run. (As if he didn't know!) It was being afraid of embarrassing Mark, or himself. It was . . . fear. Hel-lo . . . Brian the Bold was afraid! So afraid he'd never looked past the outside difference to see the *person* inside. Another kid. Just like him.

> **Brian had never looked past the outside differences to see the *person* inside.**

If he'd had a free hand, he would have slapped his own forehead. As it was, he just looked at Mark as if he were seeing him for the first time—which, in a way, he was.

"Well?" prompted Mark with a lift of one eyebrow. "I haven't got all day, you know. Gotta run."

"Uh! Oh, yeah. Thanks, man. Thanks!" And Brian stepped through the open door.

"Hey . . . wait up," he called as Mark zipped past him and away. The wheelchair obligingly slowed down, and Brian hobbled as fast as he could to catch up.

"You ever do any racing in that thing?" he asked.

"A little," said Mark—who had his sights set firmly on a wheelchair games championship. "A little. Now and then. Need to work out a better strategy, though."

"Yeah?" Brian loved to talk strategy. "What seems to be the problem?"

What must it have felt like for Jesus when he became one of us, and all the emotions of sin tumbled in on him like shadows in a forest? He felt anxious, guilty, and alone. Can't you hear those things in his prayer? "My God, my God, why have you rejected me?" (Matthew 27:46). These are not the words of a saint. This is the cry of a sinner.

And this prayer is one of the most remarkable parts of his coming. But not *the* most remarkable, because I can think of something even greater. Want to know what it is? Want to know the very coolest thing about Jesus' coming?

It's not that the One who played marbles with the stars gave it up to play marbles with marbles. Or that the One who hung the galaxies gave it up to hang doorjambs for a cranky client who wanted everything yesterday but couldn't pay for anything until tomorrow.

And it's not that Jesus, in an instant, went from needing nothing to needing air, food, a tub of hot water and salts for his tired feet, and more than anything, needing somebody—anybody—who was more concerned about where he would spend eternity than where he would spend this week's paycheck.

And it wasn't that he resisted the urge to fry the two-bit, self-appointed hall monitors of holiness who dared suggest he was doing the work of the devil.

It wasn't that he kept his cool while his dozen best friends in the world felt the heat and got out of the kitchen. Or that he gave no command to the angels who begged, "Just give the nod, Lord. One word and these demons will be deviled eggs!"

Nor was it that he refused to defend himself when blamed for every sin of every soul since Adam. Nor that he stood silent as a million guilty verdicts echoed in the halls of heaven, and the giver of light was left in the chill of a sinner's night.

Not even that after three days in a dark hole he stepped into the Easter sunrise with a smile and a swagger and a question for lowly Lucifer—"Is that your best punch?"

All of that was cool, incredibly cool. But want to know the coolest thing about the One who gave up the crown of heaven for a crown of thorns?

He did it for you.

Just for you.

... with a smile and a swagger and a question for lowly Lucifer—

The Greatest "Cover-Up" of All Time

"I Forgive You"
(God's Promise in the Nails)

> He forgave all our sins.
> He canceled the debt, which listed all the rules
> we failed to follow. He took away that record
> with its rules and nailed it to the cross.
>
> COLOSSIANS 2:13–14

> God makes people right with himself through
> their faith in Jesus Christ. This is true for all who
> believe in Christ, because all are the same. All people
> have sinned and are not good enough for God's glory.
> People are made right with God by his grace,
> which is a free gift. They are made right with God
> by being made free from sin through Jesus Christ.
>
> ROMANS 3:22–24 ICB

The "looks" began on a Tuesday. Molly noticed them, but didn't think too much of it then. She had a lot on her mind at the time. A history paper—which wasn't anywhere *near* finished—was due Friday. She still hadn't come up with a really neat service project idea for her church youth group. And she had absolutely *no* idea how she was going to convince her mom that shopping for Kim's birthday present was more important than this week's piano lesson! On the other hand, Mom *was* a huge fan of Kim's—so she might understand how incredibly *awful* it would be to miss Kim's birthday.

Molly and Kim had been best friends for years. They met in kindergarten—right after Molly and her mom had suddenly packed up and moved to this new town. Molly's mind was still spinning from the speed of the move as she peeked around the door into her new classroom. She didn't know anybody! Then a tiny girl with golden skin looked over at her, and smiled. Round blue eyes met tilted brown eyes, and it was love at first sight! Molly Craig and Kim Nakamura had been inseparable ever since.

If you saw Molly's taffy-colored curls somewhere, you could count on seeing the long fall of Kim's shining black hair close by. What one tried, the other had to do, too—

with varying degrees of success, which kept them in stitches.

Swim lessons? Kim took to the water like a fish; Molly was more of a "flounder." *Both* of them nearly drowned laughing.

An experiment with cooking? Molly's fudge was heavenly; Kim couldn't even make Jell-O.

"That's two *cups* of water, Kim, not two quarts!"

"Well . . . if you insist on reading the *directions!*" Giggle. Giggle.

Church choir? Molly made up for in enthusiasm what she lacked in pitch. So Kim sang a little louder to cover up her friend's "clinkers"—which absolutely cracked her up.

Molly and Kim. Kim and Molly. They went everywhere—did everything—together. Laughing all the way.

"Giggles, Incorporated," Molly's mom called them.

"The Dynamic Duo," said their friends.

"East meets West, and . . . look out, world!" was Mrs. Nakamura's smiling comment on the friendship.

Molly and Kim. Kim and Molly. Peas in a pod. Two sides of the same coin. Best friends. Which is what made what happened hurt so much. Cut like a knife. Pierce like a nail . . .

Busy as she was, by Friday Molly had definitely noticed the looks. How could she not?! In class, at lunch, on the soccer field . . . every time she glanced up, she caught a pair of eyes looking at *her*. Kids she knew. Kids she didn't know. Kids she'd never even seen before. And *such* looks! Pity. Curiosity. Sly enjoyment.

Even worse, when they weren't looking at her—or looking quickly away when she caught them looking—they seemed to be talking *about* her. And she couldn't begin to count the times a conversation had stopped dead when she joined a group of her friends.

It was mortifying! Everyone—everyone—seemed to know some huge secret about *her.*

But I don't have any secrets! she thought. *At least not any worth all this fuss. Except for . . . Oh, no!*

The truth was, Molly *did* have a secret. Well, it wasn't exactly *her* secret, and she hadn't known it all that long herself. But she'd promised her mother she wouldn't tell a soul. And she hadn't. Except . . . okay, it *did* just kind of slip out when she was talking to—

But Kim would never—

Would she . . . ?!

>>>>>>>>>>>>>>>>>>>>>>>>>>>>

We all have things in our lives that we'd rather no one knew about. Things, and moments, that embarrass us or make us ashamed. Now, wouldn't it be awful if someone wrote them all down—and passed them around?!

Think about it for a minute: a list of our weaknesses and mistakes and secrets. Not exactly a "fun" idea, is it? I know I don't want to think of mine making the rounds! Would you like anyone to see yours? Would you like them made public? How would you feel if they were posted high so that everyone, including Christ himself, could see?

May I take you to the moment when that really happened? Yes, there is a list of your failures. Christ has chronicled your shortcomings. Knows every mistake and secret. And, yes, that list has been made public. But you've never seen it. Neither have I. Nor has anyone else.

Come with me to the hill of Calvary, and I'll tell you why.

Watch as the soldiers shove the Carpenter to the ground and stretch his arms against the beams of the cross. One presses a knee against a forearm and a spike against a hand. Jesus turns his face toward the nail just as the soldier lifts the hammer to strike it.

Couldn't Jesus have stopped him? With a flex of the biceps, with a clench of the fist, he could have resisted. Is this not the same hand that stilled the sea? Cleansed the Temple? Summoned the dead?

But the fist doesn't clench ... and the moment isn't altered.

The hammer rings and the skin rips and the blood begins to drip, then rush. Then the questions follow. Why? Why didn't Jesus resist?

"Because he loved us," we reply. That is true, wonderfully true, but—forgive me—only partly true. There is more to his reason. He saw something that made him stay. As the soldier pressed his arm, Jesus rolled his head to the side, and with his cheek resting on the wood he saw:

A hammer? Yes.

A nail? Yes.

The soldier's hand? Yes.

But he saw something else, too. He saw the hand of God. It appeared to be the hand of a man. Long fingers of a woodworker. Calloused palm of a carpenter. It appeared common, this hand of his. It was, however, anything but.

These fingers formed Adam out of clay and furrowed truth into tablets.

With a wave, this hand toppled Babel's tower and split the Red Sea.

From this hand flew the locusts that plagued Egypt and the raven that fed Elijah.

The hand of God is a mighty hand. A loving hand. A hand about to feel the bite of a nail.

Oh, the hands of Jesus. Hands of incarnation at his birth. Hands of liberation as he healed. Hands of inspiration as he taught. Hands of dedication as he served. Hands of salvation as he died. And hands of love as he forgave.

"How could you, Kim? How could you?! You promised not to tell a soul!" Her blue eyes flashing, Molly glared at her friend. (Make that *former* friend!)

Kim's soft brown eyes were filled with tears. "Oh, Molly, I'm so sorry. Really . . . I didn't mean to. I didn't even know I was going to say it, until I . . . *said* it."

"How can something like that just slip out?!" snapped Molly, conveniently forgetting just who had been the *first* to let the secret out.

"I know. I know. It was dumb," agreed Kim. She felt just terrible about the way everyone was making such a big deal of the whole thing.

"We were talking in class about heredity—the way some things just seem to run in families," Kim tried to explain. "And I said it wasn't always true. That you were the most honest person I knew, even if you did have an uncle in prison for embezzl—"

"Class . . . ?! You talked about it in *class?!*" Molly could barely get the words out. No wonder the entire school was buzzing with the story!

"I'll never forgive you for this, Kim. *Never!*"

Shut up in her room, Molly gloomed and fumed her way through the weekend. *At least I don't have to face anyone for a couple of days,* she thought. But Monday would come, and so would more of the looks. And it was all Kim's fault. *Fine friend she is!*

In fact, the more she thought about it, the madder she got. And the more things she found about her "friend" that bugged her! The way Kim was *never* on time. All those trips to the museum, when she *knew* Molly didn't care the least little bit about art. Her refusal to ever read directions ("Oh, let's just try it and see what happens"). The really annoying way that every single long, silky black hair was always perfectly in place. And, of course, the way she broke her promise not to tell!

By Sunday night her list of Kim's flaws was very long indeed. Of course, if you wanted to be fair about the whole thing—which Molly was in *no* mood to be—you could come up with a pretty impressive Molly list, too.

After all, there wouldn't have been a secret to keep in the first place, if Molly hadn't been looking—okay, snooping—through her mother's desk. And if she hadn't opened the letter . . . and *read* it. And, of course, she'd made a promise of her own, to her mother, not to tell.

"It's family business, Molly," her mother had said when Molly finally asked her about the letter—and the uncle she barely remembered from childhood. "Not something anybody else needs to know about.

"Having a brother in prison isn't something I'm proud of. And I *hated* the way everyone talked about it . . . the looks I got. That's why we moved to this new town when you were just five. So *you* wouldn't have to live with those same looks." Her mother paused. "And what *were* you doing going through my desk anyway?" Which led to a whole other pretty uncomfortable conversation.

But not nearly as uncomfortable for Molly as the next week at school. It was every bit as miserable as she thought it would be. What made it even worse, of course, was facing it by herself.

This time there was no best friend at her side to say, "Never mind . . ."; no consoling squeeze of the hand; no reassuring "Who cares anyway?" grin to cheer her up. Because Molly was *not* speaking to Kim! Not a single word. Not one. Never again. No matter how hopefully Kim smiled at her . . . or how hurt she looked every time Molly turned and walked away.

Which gave everyone something *else* to buzz about, too. (*Molly and Kim not speaking?!*)

The week dragged on. Molly kept her chin up and tried to ignore the whispers and curious looks. And Kim? Well, Kim just seemed to "wilt" a little more each day.

Serves her right, thought Molly. *What she did was unforgivable!* But, strangely, the sad, lost look on Kim's face didn't make Molly feel the least bit better.

The crowd at the cross thought that the purpose of the pounding—the mission of the nails—was to fix the hands of Christ to a beam. But they were only half right. We can't fault them for missing the other half. They couldn't see it. But Jesus could. And heaven could. And we can—if we know where to look and what to look for.

Through the eyes of Scripture we see what others missed but what Jesus saw: "He canceled the record that contained the charges against us. He took it and destroyed it by nailing it to Christ's cross" (Colossians 2:14 NLT).

Between Jesus' hand and the wood there was a list. A long list. A list of our mistakes: our anger and lies, our spiteful thoughts and greedy moments and wasted hours. A list of our sins.

Dangling from the cross is an itemized catalog of your sins. The bad choices from last year. The bad attitudes from last week. There, in broad daylight for all of heaven to see, is a list of your mistakes. And mine.

The mistakes are covered. The sins are hidden. Those at the top are hidden by his hand; those down the list are covered by his blood. Your sins are "blotted out" by Jesus (KJV). "He has forgiven you all your sins: he has utterly wiped out the written evidence of broken commandments which always hung over our heads, and has completely annulled it by nailing it to the cross" (Colossians 2:14 PHILLIPS).

This is why he refused to close his fist. He saw the list! What kept him from resisting? This warrant, this inventory of your failures. He knew the price of those sins was death. He knew the source of those sins was you, and since he couldn't bear the thought of eternity without you, he chose the nails. He chose to forgive.

Molly's mother knew something was wrong. But she also liked to give Molly room to work things out for herself. *But enough is enough!* Thursday night—after she'd told Kim for the tenth time that week that Molly was "too busy" to come to the phone—she marched upstairs to Molly's room.

"What's up, Moll? What's going on with you and Kim?"

"Going on? Noth—Oh, Mom, it's such a mess! I don't know what to do . . ." And the whole story came pouring out. Along with more than a few tears.

"Okay," said her mother with a sigh. "Okay! First of all, it's not the end of the world, even though I once thought so, too. But I've learned you can't stop people from talking about you, if they're determined to do that. The kids at school will soon find something else to gossip about. By next month, this will all be old news."

"But it's so . . . embarrassing!"

"Yes," her mother agreed, handing Molly another tissue, "it is. Trust me, I know how it feels. But that's not what's *really* bothering you, is it?"

Molly wiped away a stray tear. "You're right," she said with a sigh. "It's Kim and me. She's miserable. I'm miserable. And I don't know what to d-d-do!"

Mrs. Craig smiled then gave her daughter a hug. "Well, you *could* forgive her."

"Forgive her?!" came the indignant answer. "But she told . . . and she promised she never would!"

"Kind of like *you* did?"

"But that's diff—" Molly interrupted herself. "Oh! . . ."

If things hadn't been so serious right then, her mother would have laughed at the look on Molly's face. Instead, she quietly said, "You know, someone else has *already* forgiven a lot of people for a lot *more* than just a slip of the tongue. *And* taught us all how to do it. Or haven't you been paying attention in Sunday school?"

Molly's blue eyes started to shine, then she jumped up and dashed downstairs to the phone. She was just about to punch in Kim's number when she had an *awful* thought.

"But what if she won't forgive *me*?" she yelled up the stairs.

"Oh, I wouldn't worry about that. Forgiveness can be a *very* contagious thing!" her mother said.

When you look at the cross—when your eyes linger on the broken hands and the cruel nails—remember this:

- *The hand squeezing the handle was not a Roman infantryman.*
- *The force behind the hammer was not an angry mob.*
- *The verdict behind the death was not decided by jealous Jews.*
- *Jesus himself chose the nails.*

So the hands of Jesus opened up. Had the soldier hesitated, Jesus himself would have swung the hammer. He knew how; he was no stranger to the driving of nails. As a carpenter he knew what it took. And as a Savior he knew what it meant. He knew that the real purpose of the nail was to place your sins where they could be hidden by his sacrifice and covered by his blood. And forgiven.

- *So Jesus himself swung the hammer.*
- *The same hand that stills the seas stills your guilt.*
- *The same hand that cleansed the Temple cleanses your heart.*
- *The hand is the hand of God.*
- *The nail is the nail of God.*

And as the hands of Jesus opened for the nail, the doors of heaven opened for you. Because you were forgiven.

...The doors of heaven opened for you.

53

5

Sometimes a Shout . . .
Sometimes a Whisper

"I Will Speak to You in Your Language"
(God's Promise Through the Sign)

Pilate wrote a sign and put it on the cross.
It read: "JESUS OF NAZARETH, THE KING OF THE JEWS."

JOHN 19:19 ICB

So faith comes from hearing the Good News.
And people hear the Good News when
someone tells them about Christ.

ROMANS 10:17 ICB

Signs

Ever had your mom go ballistic over your messy room—and been totally amazed that it was such a big deal with her? Even though she *had* mentioned it one or two—or ten—times? Rolled her eyes every time she looked in? Finally posted a "CONDEMNED" notice on your door?

You missed the signs.

Or maybe you've taken a header on your skateboard, when a wheel flew off during a critical move. You know, that wheel that had been squeaking and wobbling for weeks. . . .

You missed the signs.

Sometimes we all miss the signs. The framer of our destiny is familiar with our denseness. God knows we sometimes miss the signs. Maybe that's why he has given us so many. The rainbow after the flood signifies God's covenant. A single star over Bethlehem announced the birth of God's son, and all the stars of heaven portray the size of his family. Communion is a sign of his death, and baptism is a sign of our spiritual birth. Each of these signs symbolizes a greater spiritual truth.

But the most heart-touching—the most *telling*—sign is one you may never have thought about at all: the sign on the cross. A few hasty, handwritten words on a scrap of wood. So common. So ordinary. So easy to overlook. Just like some people. . . .

It was easy to overlook David. He made sure of that.

When you're shorter, thinner, quieter—just plain *littler*—than everyone else your age, "keeping a low profile" isn't just a phrase. It's a fact of life! It was also, as far as David was concerned, a *very* good idea.

The truth was: David was shy. Really shy. Very, very shy. Compared to David, a mouse was as bold as a lion. Compared to David, a sparrow was as flashy as a peacock. Compared to David—

Not that anyone ever *did* compare anything to David. Before you can compare, first you have to notice. And by the time David reached eighth grade his Invisible Man routine was nearly perfect. Which suited him just fine. Sort of. Most of the time.

Of course, not everyone missed him. Emma Johnson always had a sweet smile and a friendly "Hi, David!" for him. David just blushed.

And Zack Porter was really nice when he crashed into David in the crowded hallway just before third bell. "Sorry, man. Didn't see you. You okay?" He rescued David's glasses from a descending foot, and even helped gather up ten (!) scattered books. "Wow, you sure must like to read."

"Uh . . . yes . . . I do," mumbled David. Which was something of an understatement.

David didn't just like to read . . . he *loved* to read. In fact, David didn't just read . . . he *devoured* books. Jumped right inside. Wrapped himself up in every story. You might say that David lived his life in books. In books, he wasn't shy, quiet little David—who never had the least idea what to say or do around his bigger, faster, *noisier* classmates. In books, David roamed galaxies, fought dragons, climbed mountains, saved the day, and always—always—said exactly the right thing. In books, David was a hero!

Of course, there wasn't the slightest sign of any of that on the outside. At first glance, you might think you knew all there was to know about David. And David himself would be the last person to think he might be a hero in "real life." But that was about to change. . . .

The sign on the cross seems easy enough to understand, too—at first glance. You know the story:

> Pilate wrote a sign and put it on the cross. It read: "JESUS OF
> NAZARETH, THE KING OF THE JEWS." The sign was written in the
> Jewish language, in Latin, and in Greek. Many of the Jews read
> the sign, because this place where Jesus was killed was near
> the city. The leading Jewish priests said to Pilate, "Don't write,
> 'The King of the Jews.' But write, 'This man said, I am the King
> of the Jews.'"
>
> Pilate answered, "What I have written, I have written!"
> (John 19:19–22 ICB)

Yes, pretty simple stuff. A hand-painted, Roman-ordered sign, in three languages. Almost an afterthought on Pilate's part. That's *what* it was. But it's the *whys* that hold the clues:

Why is a sign placed over the head of Jesus in the first place? Why does its wording trouble the Jews, and why does Pilate refuse to change it? Why are the words written in three languages, and why is the sign mentioned in all four Gospels?

Why?

Could it be that this piece of wood is a picture of God's devotion? A symbol of his passion to tell the world about his Son? A reminder that God will do whatever it takes to share with you the message of this sign? I suggest that the sign reveals two truths about God's desire to reach the world. Here's the first:

...the sign reveals two truths about God's desire to reach the world.

There is no person he will not use.

Please note that the sign on the cross bears immediate fruit. Remember the words of the criminal hanging next to Jesus? Moments from his own death, drowning in pain, he turns and says, "Jesus, remember me when you come into your kingdom" (Luke 23:42).

What an interesting choice of words. He doesn't plead, "Save me." He doesn't beg, "Have mercy on my soul." He speaks as a servant to a king. Why? Why does he refer to Jesus' kingdom? Perhaps he had heard Jesus speak. Maybe he was familiar with Jesus' words about the kingdom of heaven. Or, maybe—just maybe—he read the sign: "Jesus of Nazareth, the King of the Jews."

The thief knows he is in a royal mess. He turns his head and reads a royal proclamation and asks for royal help. It might have been this simple. If so, the sign was the first tool used to proclaim the message of the cross! And because of the sign, a soul was saved. All because someone posted a sign on a cross.

I don't know if the angels do entrance interviews in heaven. But if they do, this one would have been fun to witness. Imagine the thief arriving at the Pearly Gates Processing Center.

ANGEL: *Have a seat. Now, tell me, Mr. . . . uh . . . Thief, how did you come to be saved?*

THIEF: *I just asked Jesus to remember me in his kingdom. Sure didn't expect it to happen so quickly.*

ANGEL: *I see. And just how did you know he was a king?*

THIEF: *There was a sign over his head: "Jesus of Nazareth, the king of the Jews." I believed the sign and—here I am!*

ANGEL: *(Taking notes on a pad) Believed . . . a . . . sign.*

THIEF: *That's right. The sign was put there by some guy named John.*

ANGEL: *Don't think so.*

THIEF: *Hmmm. Maybe it was that other follower, Peter.*

ANGEL: *Nope, wasn't Peter.*

THIEF: Then which apostle did it?

ANGEL: Well, if you really want to know, the sign was Pilate's idea.

THIEF: No kidding? Pilate, huh?

ANGEL: Don't be surprised. God used a bush to call Moses and a donkey to convince a prophet. To get Jonah's attention, God used a big fish. There is no thing and no person he won't use. Well, that about wraps it up. (Stamps paper) Take this to the next window. (Thief begins to exit) Just follow the signs.

Pilate did not intend to spread the gospel. In fact, what the sign said as far as *he* was concerned was, "This is what becomes of a Jewish king; this is what the Romans do with him. The king of this nation is a slave; a crucified criminal; and if such be the king, what must the nation be whose king he is?"* Pilate had intended the sign to threaten and mock the Jews. But God had another purpose . . . Pilate was God's instrument for spreading the gospel. Unknown to himself, he was a "ghostwriter" for heaven. He took dictation from God and wrote it on a sign. And the sign changed the destiny of a reader.

It happens, you know.

---

* Isabel McHugh and Florence McHugh, trans., *The Trial of Jesus: The Jewish and Roman Proceedings against Jesus Christ Described and Assessed from the Oldest Accounts*, by Josef Blinzler (Westminster, Md.: The Newman Press, 1959), 103.

David had no idea that Mr. Hamilton (and certainly not *God!*) had something special in mind for him as he was leaving English class that Thursday.

"Hold up a minute, David," Mr. Hamilton called. "I need some help on a project that's right up your alley."

"*My* alley?!" David wasn't aware he *had* an alley.

"Yup," came the cheerful reply. (Mr. Hamilton was one of the few people who not only noticed David, but actually *saw* how much he had to offer.)

"You have a wonderful imagination, David, and a real talent for words. And I don't know anyone who appreciates the power of books more than you do. How 'bout sharing those gifts?"

Sharing? What . . . With whom . . . ?! David had no idea what Mr. Hamilton was talking about.

"Here's the deal, David. A group of us are trying to start a Reading Mentor program for some younger kids who need a hand. Kids without a lot of hope in their lives.

"Did you know there are third and fourth graders who can barely read?! Every word—every day in school—is a struggle. And every day they fall a little farther behind. Think what that must feel like."

Good as his imagination was, David could barely picture it. To walk into class every day and open a book that made no sense? To wrestle with *every* word? To have no idea what was even *on* page 38—never mind writing a report about it!

Why, you'd never *keep up. Or catch up. So you'd probably just . . . give up!* David had to admit: It would be awful. But he didn't see what it had to do with him.

But Mr. Hamilton did. "So here's what we thought . . .
What if we got big kids to help little kids work on their reading?" (*Big*? David's lips twitched.) "Teens they could look up
to." David nearly smiled. "Someone to encourage them,
someone who understands the *magic* of words. Someone
like . . . you."

Two months later, David still wasn't quite sure how he
ended up—every Wednesday after school—in this room, sitting next to Jason, with a book. He was pretty sure he hadn't
exactly said yes to Mr. Hamilton. On the other hand, a whispered no is pretty easy to ignore.

Actually, it wasn't so bad—although the first few times had
been a little hairy. For one thing, his "little kid" was not so little.
Nine-year-old Jason was at least two inches taller than David.
And, boy, did he have a mouth on him. Jason had an opinion
on everything! And he wasn't all that thrilled at being here.

"What good's reading gonna do me anyway?"

But David had an answer for that one. "Depends on where
you want to go."

"What's that mean—'where I want to go'?" Jason shot back.

"Well," said David, "ever been to Mars?"

"Mars?!" hooted Jason. "Man, I've never been out of my
'hood!"

"A book can take you there," David assured him. "Or to
the top of Mount Everest. Or the bottom of the sea—"

"Yeah . . . ?" Jason looked kind of interested.

"In a flash," said David, grinning. "Of course, *first*, you have to be able to read it."

Jason thought that over a bit. Then asked, "What about hockey?"

"Hockey?" David wasn't exactly a big sports fan.

"Yeah! There a book about hockey? Something with Wayne Gretzky in it? Man, he's the greatest!"

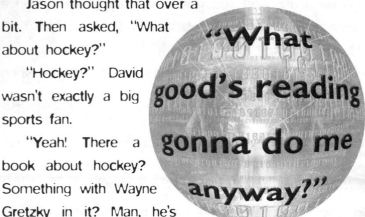

"Uh . . . ," said David, "I'm sure there is. Got to be. Next week," he promised.

And sure enough, there was a hockey book on Gretzky. And it was a big success. Sort of sucked Jason into the *fun* of reading. And so it went. Every time Jason got discouraged—and he did—David found a new way (and the right words) to keep him going. Not that it was easy. But David knew he had something Jason needed, and if talking was what it took . . . *Okay, I'll talk!*

Best of all was the time David asked, "If you could be anything in the world you wanted to, what would you be?"

Jason shrugged. Then he laughed. "You mean like an astronaut, or a . . . a doctor?! Man, you must be nuts! I could never be one of those things."

"Why not?" asked David, perfectly serious. "Who—besides *you*—says you can't?"

Jason was still laughing. "Where'd I get the money for something like that? And you gotta be really smart . . ." He shook his head. "All kinds of ob-sta-cles (a new word he'd just mastered that day)."

"Well," said David, "what does Wayne Gretzky do when something gets in *his* way?"

Jason just stared at David for a long time. Then he kind of looked *through* David, with a very strange expression on his face. Like someone who had opened a door he didn't know was there—and had seen something wonderful.

Then Jason started to smile—and grabbed the book he'd been struggling with. "Well?" he demanded. "What are we waiting for? Got us a lot of work to do. . . ."

The power of words. A thief is led to Christ by Pilate who rejected Christ. A kid with a lot of attitude and not much future has his world changed by a shy kid who never dreamed he had so *much* to say. It happens, you know.

There is no person God will not use. Remember? That's the *first* truth revealed by the sign on the cross. Here's the second truth:

There is no language God will not speak.

Every passerby could read the sign on the cross, because every passerby could read Hebrew (the Jewish language), Latin, or Greek—

the three great languages of the ancient world. "Hebrew was the language of Israel, the language of religion; Latin the language of the Romans, the language of law and government; and Greek the language of Greece, the language of culture. Christ was declared king in them all."* God had a message for each: "Christ is king." The message was the same, but the languages were different. Since Jesus was a King for all people, the message would be in the tongues of all people.

There is no language God will not speak. Which leads us to a delightful question: What language is he speaking to *you?* What clues does he hide in the day-to-day drama of *your* life? God does speak, you know. He speaks to us in whatever language we will understand. And not always in words.

There are times he speaks the language of "plenty." Is your tummy full? Do you have cool clothes to wear? Got a little jingle in your pocket? Feels good, doesn't it? But be careful: Don't be so proud of what you have that you miss the *rest* of the message. Could it be that you have much so you can give much? "God can give you more blessings than you need. Then you will always have plenty of everything—enough to give to every good work" (2 Corinthians 9:8).

Is God speaking to you in the language of "plenty"? Pretty nice, isn't it? But, you know, sometimes God has something to say to us in *other* ways. Sometimes we may *not* have everything we need—or think we need. Sometimes we bump headlong into a pretty big challenge (which is also another name for "opportunity"). And every once in a while we find ourselves in situations that make us really uncomfortable. And we have no idea how we got there. Or why. Or what the point is.

* McHugh and McHugh, *The Trial of Jesus*, 104.

But God knows. And works in our lives—with loving care—every day. All we really have to do is pay attention.

David sat in homeroom, smiling to himself, not really hearing the noisy discussion going on around him. He could still see the pride in Jason's eyes yesterday when the boy showed his mentor a test paper. A big, fat B! (Jason had never had one of *those* before.) Amazing! The look on his face made David feel ten feet tall. Well . . . almost.

Then Emma stood up, and David started paying attention. "Come on, guys," she said, "we can do better than this. Doesn't anybody have any really *terrific* ideas for our service project?"

David had absolutely no idea how he ended up on his feet. "Uh . . . ," he said.

Everything stopped. Every head turned. *David? David had something to say?!*

David very nearly sat right back down. *No! Not this time. This is too important. We need more volunteers!*

"Uh . . ." David cleared his throat. "I've got one." His voice shook only a tiny bit. "An idea. . . ." He cleared his throat again. "Let me tell you about Jason . . ."

You could have heard a pin drop while David—shy, quiet David—told his story. Then everyone talked at once. They loved the idea! And they were all smiling . . . at *him*.

"It's a *wonderful* idea, David." Emma beamed—as every kid in the room signed up for "Jasons" of their own.

"Wow," chimed in a very impressed Zack, "who would've guessed?!"

As he did with the sign on the cross, God speaks to each of us in the language we need to hear.

For David, it was the books he'd hidden in that God used to launch him into the real world. And show him that he had something special to do there, too.

For Jason, it was the reading he'd struggled with that God used to give him the key to a future he'd never imagined.

And the kids in David's class? Well, it *could* be that God was using David to remind them that things, *and* people, might not be quite so ordinary as they seem—at first glance.

Or, as Zack (who loved clichés) put it: "You sure can't judge a book by its cover!"

God speaks to each of us in exactly the way that will reach us best. He could be talking to you right now.

God has a special plan for *your* life—*your* gifts—and he tells you about it in many ways. Sometimes he shouts ... *sometimes* he whispers.

Are you listening?

God speaks to each of us in the language we need to hear.

6

Be Careful What You Ask For: You Might Get It!

"I Will Let You Choose"
(God's Promise Through the Two Crosses)

There they nailed Jesus to the cross. They also put two other men on crosses, one on each side of Jesus with Jesus in the middle.

JOHN 19:18 ICB

There's someone I'd like you to meet: a very famous actor named Edwin Thomas. He—

Who? Edwin Thomas?! Never heard of him, right? Trust me, he was a superstar. The Mel Gibson . . . the Harrison Ford . . . of his day. (Of course, his "day" *was* in the 1800s—a little before your time maybe. Even before *my* time!)

Edwin made his stage debut at the age of fifteen in *Richard III*, and quickly became known as one of the finest Shakespearean actors of the time. They raved about him in New York . . . loved him in London! When it came to tragedy on the stage, Edwin Thomas was in a very select group.

When it came to tragedy in life, the same thing was true.

Edwin had two brothers, John and Junius. Both were actors, too, though neither could match Edwin's talent. In 1863, the three brothers appeared together in *Julius Caesar*. Edwin's brother John played the role of Brutus. Which would have sent a shiver up the spines of the audience, had they known what awaited the brothers—and the nation—two years later.

For this John who played the stage assassin in *Julius Caesar* is the same John who took the role of real-life assassin in Ford's Theatre. On a crisp April night in 1865, he stole quietly into the rear of a box in the Washington, D.C., theater and fired a bullet into the head of President Abraham Lincoln.

Yes, the last name of the brothers was Booth—Edwin Thomas Booth and John Wilkes Booth.

Edwin was never the same after that night. Shame from his brother's crime drove him into retirement. He might never have returned to the stage had it not been for a twist of fate at a New Jersey train station. Edwin was waiting for his coach when a well-dressed young man, pushed by the crowd, lost his footing and fell between the platform and a moving train. Without hesitation, Edwin locked a leg around a railing, grabbed the man, and pulled him to safety. After the sighs of relief, the young man recognized the famous Edwin Booth.

Edwin, however, didn't recognize the young man he'd rescued. That knowledge came weeks later in a letter. A letter he carried in his pocket for the rest of his life. A letter from General Ulysses S. Grant's secretary. A letter thanking Edwin Booth for saving the life of the child of an American hero—Abraham Lincoln!

Strange, isn't it? One brother killed the president; the other brother saved the president's son. The boy Edwin Booth yanked to safety? Robert Todd Lincoln.*

Edwin and James Booth. Same father, mother, profession, and passion—yet one chooses life, the other, death. How could it

Abel chooses God. Cain chooses murder. And God lets him.

---

* Paul Aurandt, *Paul Harvey's the Rest of the Story* (New York: Bantam Press, 1977), 47.

happen? I don't know, but it does. Though their story is dramatic, it's not unique.

Abel and Cain, both sons of Adam. Abel chooses God. Cain chooses murder. And God lets him.

Abraham and Lot, both pilgrims in Canaan. Abraham chooses God. Lot chooses Sodom. And God lets him.

David and Saul, both kings of Israel. David chooses God. Saul chooses power. And God lets him.

Peter and Judas, both deny their Lord. Peter seeks mercy. Judas seeks death. And God lets him.

In every age of history, on every page of Scripture, the truth is revealed: God allows us to make our own choices!

And no one says this more clearly than Jesus. According to him:

We can choose:

⊠ *a narrow gate or a wide gate (Matthew 7:13–14)*

⊠ *an easy road or a hard road (Matthew 7:13–14)*

⊠ *the big crowd or the small crowd (Matthew 7:13–14)*

We can choose to:

⊠ *build on rock or sand (Matthew 7:24–27)*

⊠ *serve God or riches (Matthew 6:24)*

⊠ *be numbered among the sheep or the goats (Matthew 25:32–33)*

"These people [those who rejected God] will go off to be punished forever. But the good people will go to live forever" (Matthew
25:46 ICB).

God gives eternal choices, and these choices have eternal consequences.

All Michael—Mike!—O'Hara wanted was to belong . . . to
be part of something . . . to have friends. Was that asking
too much, for heaven's sake?!

And he'd found some—which wasn't at all easy for a kid
starting high school. And these guys were really cool. Yes,
they were! So what if a lot of the other kids at school seemed
to . . . avoid . . . them?! He didn't notice any of *those* kids
rushing over to say "Hi!" or make him feel welcome, which
was fine with him. Mike had found his own friends. Or they
found him. Take your choice.

Who'd have dreamed that an afternoon at the mall—just
hanging out with his buddies—would turn out to be so . . .
complicated?! Or bring Mike face-to-face with such an enormous choice?

God gives eternal choices, and these choices have eternal consequences. It's a thought worth repeating . . . and remembering.

Isn't this the reminder of the three crosses of Calvary? Ever wonder why there were two crosses next to Jesus? Why not six or ten? Ever wonder why Jesus was in the center? Why not on the far right or far left? Could it be that the two crosses on the hill symbolize one of God's greatest gifts? The gift of choice.

The two criminals crucified with Jesus have so much in common. Convicted by the same system. Condemned to the same death. Surrounded by the same crowd. Equally close to Jesus. In fact, they begin with the same attitude that day at Calvary: "The two criminals also said cruel things to Jesus" (Matthew 27:44 CEV).

But one changed.

> One of the criminals on a cross began to shout insults at Jesus: "Aren't you the Christ? Then save yourself and us." But the other criminal stopped him and said, "You should fear God! You are getting the same punishment he is. We are punished justly, getting what we deserve for what we did. But this man has done nothing wrong." Then he said, "Jesus, remember me when you come into your kingdom." Jesus said to him, "I tell you the truth, today you will be with me in paradise."
> (Luke 23:39–43)

Much has been said about the prayer of the penitent thief, and it certainly deserves our admiration. But while we rejoice at the thief who changed, dare we forget the one who didn't? *What about him, Jesus? Wouldn't a personal invitation be appropriate? Wouldn't a word of persuasion be timely? We don't understand!*

Does not the shepherd leave the ninety-nine sheep and pursue the one lost? Does not the housewife sweep the house until the lost coin is found?

Yes, the shepherd does, the housewife does, but the father of the prodigal, remember, does nothing.

The sheep was lost innocently.

The coin was lost accidentally.

But the prodigal son left intentionally.

The father gave him the choice. Jesus gave both criminals the same. He let them choose. Just as he lets *us* choose. Just as he let Mike choose . . .

Laughing, shoving—taking up twice as much space as they needed—the noisy group of boys strutted through the mall. Right in the middle was Mike—trying really hard to look as bold and confident as they all did. And why shouldn't he? He belonged. He had friends!

Well, sure, some of the things they did felt just a little . . . risky. And climbing out his window to join one of their "midnight rambles" wasn't quite as much fun as he'd thought it would be. But what did they do that was so awful, anyway? Dumping over a few trash cans . . . setting off car alarms? Not such a big deal! (Jay wasn't *really* trying to break into those cars. Just kidding around. *Wasn't he?!*)

Hey, cut 'em some slack, they're your friends!

And they *were* his friends. Good friends. Mike just wished some of the things they came up with for him to do didn't feel so much like a . . . *test.* And that maybe his parents liked them a little bit better. He'd heard them talking last night when they thought he was asleep.

> ". . . I just know those boys are headed for trouble. And taking Michael right along with them!" That was his mom.
>
> His dad wasn't quite so bent out of shape. "Aw, they're just kids, Katie. Noisy, *cocky* kids, I'll admit. And I'm not so sure, either, that they're the best friends for Mike. But life is full of choices, and we can't follow him around and make them for him. Mike's got a good head on his shoulders. He'll figure it out."

Figure what *out?* wondered Mike, as he walked right into Jay—who had stopped walking entirely. Who was just standing there. Staring thoughtfully into the window of the music store.

"Hey, watch it, man!"

"Oh, . . . sorry, Jay. Wasn't thinking." (Were those *cigarettes* in Jay's pocket? Man, he sure didn't want to go *there.* Those things could kill you!)

"No problem," said Jay, "we're friends, right?" Then he grinned and looked around at the other guys, who grinned back.

"Hey, Mike!" said Kyle, "bet that new CD you've been wanting is right inside this store. Just waiting for you to pick it up." And everybody laughed.

Mike smiled back, not really sure what was so funny. "Don't I wish! However, there's this little problem of cash—"

"Hey, who said anything about *buying* it?" asked Jay with a challenging look.

That took a bit to sink in. Then the light dawned. *They want me to steal that CD!* Mike just stared at them all. And they stared right back. Daring him *not* to.

"Just think of it as your 'entrance exam,' kid," said Jay. "Unless you're gonna wimp out on us . . . ? Up to you . . ."

Mike was too stunned to say a word. He just stood there in the silence that grew longer . . . and longer.

There are times when God sends thunder to stir us. There are times when God sends blessings to lure us. But then there are times when God sends nothing but silence as he honors us with the freedom to *choose* where we spend eternity.

And what an honor it is! In so many areas of life we have no choice. Think about it. You didn't choose your gender. You didn't choose your siblings. You didn't choose your race or place of birth.

Sometimes our lack of choices angers us. "It's not fair," we say. "It's not fair that I was born poor or that I sing so badly or that I run so slowly." But the scales of life were forever tipped on the side of fairness when God planted a tree in the Garden of Eden. All complaints were silenced when Adam and his descendants were given free will—the freedom to make whatever eternal choice we desire.

Any injustice in this life is offset by the honor of choosing our destiny in the next.

Wouldn't you agree? Would you have wanted otherwise? Would you have preferred the opposite? You choose everything in this life, and he chooses where you spend the next? You choose the size of your nose, the color of your hair, and he chooses where you spend eternity? Is that what you would prefer?

It would have been nice if God had let us order life like we order a meal. I'll take good health and a high IQ. I'll pass on the music skills, but give me lots of friends...Would've been nice. But it didn't happen. When it came to your life on earth, you weren't given a choice or a vote.

... God sends thunder to stir us.

But when it comes to life after death, you are given a choice. In my book that seems like a good deal. Wouldn't you agree?

Have we been given any greater privilege than that of choice? Not only does this privilege offset any injustice, the gift of free will can offset any mistakes.

Think about the thief who repented. Though we know little about him, we know this: He made some bad mistakes in life. He chose the wrong crowd, the wrong morals, the wrong behavior. But would you consider his life a waste? Is he spending eternity reaping the fruit of all the bad choices he made? No, just the opposite. He is enjoying the fruit of the one good choice he made. In the end all his bad choices were redeemed by a solitary good one.

You've made some bad choices in life, haven't you? Maybe you've chosen the wrong friends, or the wrong goals . . . made all kinds of decisions you wish you hadn't. You look back and say, "If only . . . if only I could make up for those bad choices." You can. One good choice for eternity offsets a thousand bad ones on earth.

The choice is yours.

How can two brothers be born of the same mother, grow up in the same home, and one choose life and the other choose death? I don't know, but they do.

How could two men see the same Jesus and one choose to mock him and the other choose to pray to him? I don't know, but they did.

And when one prayed, Jesus loved him enough to save him. And when the other mocked, Jesus loved him enough to let him.

He allowed him the choice.

He does the same for you.

Mike's mind was racing as he stood there, looking through the window of the music store.

It would be so easy. The store was crowded. The clerks were busy. He was quick. And there were so *many* CDs. Who'd miss just one?

It would be so easy. A lot of kids did it. And no one—

besides his friends—would ever know. Well . . . *one* other person would know. Mike would.

Which made all the difference. Friends are important—and he desperately wanted these guys for friends—but so is being able to look yourself in the eye in the mirror and not be ashamed.

And then there was that thing his dad always said, too. His proud, *honest* dad, who worked so hard to take care of his family. And felt so bad when there were things he couldn't give them. "We may not have a lot, Mike, but what we do have is truly ours. Because every bit of it is honestly *earned*."

Yeah, it would *be easy. But once you start down* that *road . . .*

"Well?" prodded Jay. "You in or you out? Your choice."

Mike straightened his shoulders and looked Jay—laughing, daredevil Jay—right in the eye. "Yes, it is *MY* choice."

He took one last regretful look at these friends he liked so much—who were headed in a direction that was not for him. "Sorry, guys, just not my thing. See you around."

Then Mike turned and walked away.

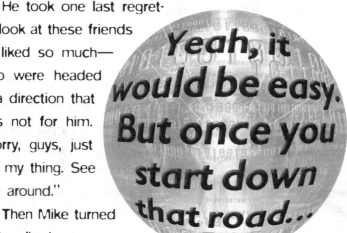

Yeah, it would be easy. But once you start down that road...

7

If You Don't Know Where You're Going, You Might End Up Somewhere Else!
—YOGI BERRA

"I Will Not Abandon You"
(God's Promise in the Path to Calvary)

*And not only that, but now we are also
very happy in God through our Lord Jesus Christ.
Through Jesus we are now God's friends again.*

ROMANS 5:11 ICB

*God made us free from
the power of darkness, and he brought us
into the kingdom of his dear Son.*

COLOSSIANS 1:13 ICB

Five-year-old Madeline climbed onto her father's knee.

"Did you have enough to eat, Maddy?" he asked her.

She smiled and patted her tummy. "I can't eat any more."

"Did you have some of your grandma's pie?"

"A whole piece!"

Joe looked across the table at his mom, and winked. "Looks like you filled us up. Don't think we'll be able to do anything tonight but go to bed."

Madeline put her little hands on either side of his big face. "Oh, but, Poppa, this is Christmas Eve. You said we could dance."

Joe pretended he had a poor memory. "Did I now? Why, I don't remember saying anything about dancing."

Grandma smiled and shook her head as she began clearing the table.

"But, Poppa," Madeline pleaded, "we always dance on Christmas Eve. Just you and me, remember?"

A smile burst from beneath his thick mustache. "Of course I remember, darling. How could I forget?"

Then he stood and took her hand in his, and for a moment—just a moment—his wife was alive again. And the

two of them were walking into the den to spend another
night before Christmas as they had spent so many. Dancing
away the evening.

Joe and his wife would have danced together the rest of
their lives, but then came the surprise pregnancy and the terrible complications. Madeline—his baby, Maddy—lived. But her
beautiful mother did not. And Joe was left to raise his
Madeline alone.

"Come on, Poppa." She tugged on his hand. "Let's dance
before everyone gets here." She was right. Soon the doorbell
would ring and the relatives would fill the house and the night
would be past.

But, for now, it was just Poppa and Madeline.

The love of a parent for a child is a mighty force. Consider the couple
with their newborn child. The baby offers his parents absolutely nothing. No money. No skill. No words of wisdom. If he had pockets, they
would be empty. To see an infant lying in a bassinet is to see utter
helplessness. What is there to love?

Whatever it is, Mom and Dad find it. Just look at Mom's face as
she cuddles her baby. Just watch Dad's eyes as he holds his child. And
just try to harm or speak evil of the infant. If you do, you'll encounter
a mighty strength, for the love of a parent is a mighty force.

Jesus once asked, if we humans who are sinful have such a love,
how much more does God, our sinless and selfless Father, love us?

(see Matthew 7:11). But what happens when the love isn't returned? What happens to the heart of the father when his child turns away?

Rebellion flew into Maddy's heart—and Joe's world—like a bitter winter blizzard. About the time she was nearly old enough to drive, Madeline decided she was old enough to lead her own life. And that life did not include her father.

"I should have seen it coming," Joe would later say, "but for the life of me I didn't. Maddy always had a mind of her own. But I never expected this . . ."

He didn't know what to do. He didn't know how to handle the pierced nose and the too-short, too-tight skirts. He didn't understand the late nights and the poor grades. And, most of all, he didn't know when to speak and when to be quiet.

Madeline, on the other hand, had it all figured out. She knew when to speak to her father—never. She knew when to be quiet—always. All her words and smiles and thoughts were for the scrawny, tattooed kid who lived down the street—but he was no good, and Joe knew it.

And there was no way he was going to allow his daughter to spend Christmas Eve with that kid!

"You'll be with us tonight, young lady. You'll be at your grandma's house eating your grandma's pie. You'll be with us on Christmas Eve."

And she was. But though they were at the same table, they might as well have been on different sides of town.

Madeline played with her food and said nothing. Grandma tried to talk to Joe, but he was in no mood to chat. Part of him was angry; part of him was heartbroken. And the rest of him would have given anything to know how to talk to this girl who once sat on his knee.

Soon the relatives arrived, bringing with them a welcome end to the awkward silence. As the room filled with noise and people, Joe stayed on one side, Madeline sat sullenly on the other.

"Put on the music, Joe," reminded one of his brothers. And so he did. Thinking she would be honored, he turned and walked toward his daughter. "Will you dance with your poppa tonight?"

The way she huffed and turned away, you'd have thought he'd insulted her. In full view of the family, she walked out the front door and marched down the street. Leaving her father alone.

Very much alone.

The most notorious street in the world is the Via Dolorosa, "the Way of Sorrows." According to tradition, it is the route Jesus took from Pilate's hall to Calvary. The path is marked by "stations" often used by Christians for their devotions. One station marks the passing of Pilate's judgment. Another, the place where Simon helped Jesus carry his cross. Two stations commemorate the stumble of Christ, another the words of Christ. There are fourteen stations in all, each one a reminder of the events of Christ's final journey.

Is the route accurate? Probably not. When Jerusalem was destroyed in A.D. 70 and again in A.D. 135, the streets of the city were destroyed, too. So no one knows for sure the exact path Jesus followed that Friday.

But we do know where that path actually *began*.

The path began, not in the court of Pilate, but in the halls of heaven. The Father began the journey when he left his home in search of us. Armed with nothing more than a passion to win your heart, he came looking. He had one desire—to bring his children home. The Bible has a word for this quest: *reconciliation*.

"God was in Christ reconciling the world to Himself" (2 Corinthians 5:19 NKJV). The Greek word for *reconcile* means "to render something otherwise."* To change a thing. Make it different from what it was.

Reconciliation restitches what is unraveled. Reverses rebellion. Rekindles the cold heart with the fire of love.

Reconciliation touches the shoulder of the wayward child, and woos him homeward.

The path to the cross tells us exactly how far God will go to call us back to him.

---

* Frank Stagg, *New Testament Theology* (Nashville; Broadman Press, 1962), 102.

That scrawny boy from down the street—the one who had all Maddy's heart and attention—had a cousin. The cousin worked the night shift at a convenience store south of Houston—a world, and a long bus ride, away from the home Maddy no longer wanted. For a few bucks a month, he would let the two runaways stay in his apartment at night. But they had to be out during the day.

Which was fine with them. They had big plans. He was going to be a mechanic, and Madeline just knew she could get a job at a department store. Of course, he knew almost nothing about cars—and she knew even less about getting a job. But you don't think of things like that when you're caught up in the idea of "freedom."

Madeline found herself facing the night with no place to sleep...

After a couple of weeks, the cousin changed his mind. "Just not working out." And the day he announced his decision, the boyfriend announced his, too. Madeline found herself facing the night with no place to sleep or hand to hold.

It was the first of many such nights.

A woman in the park told her about a homeless shelter near the bridge. For a couple of bucks she could get a bowl of soup and a cot. A couple of bucks was about all she had. She used her backpack as a pillow and her jacket as a blanket.

The room was so rowdy it was hard to sleep. Madeline turned her face to the wall and, for the first time in several days, thought of the whiskered face of her father as he used to kiss her good night. But as her eyes began to water, she refused to cry. She pushed the memory deep inside and made up her mind not to think about home.

She'd gone too far to go back.

The next morning an older girl in the cot beside her showed her a fistful of tips she'd made from dancing in a nightclub. "This is the last night I'll have to stay here," she said. "Now I can pay for my own place."

She took a second look at Madeline's pretty face and slender body. "You know, you should try it. I know they're looking for another girl. And they're not too fussy about age—as long as you don't mind being looked at. And know how to dance." She reached into her pocket and pulled out a matchbook. "Here's the address, if you're interested."

Madeline's stomach sort of turned over at the thought. All she could do was mumble, "I'll . . . I'll think about it."

Dance in a nightclub . . . while people watched?! I'd rather starve!

She spent the rest of the week on the streets looking for work. But there weren't any jobs for underage girls with no references. And she was too proud—and embarrassed—to go up to strangers and ask for money, the way a lot of runaways did.

Something will turn up. I know it will!

At the end of the week it was time to pay her bill at the

shelter. She reached into her pocket—and pulled out the matchbook. It was all she had left.

"I won't be staying tonight," she said, and walked out the door.

Madeline didn't know where she was going to go. Or what she was going to do. She only knew where she *couldn't* go, and what she *couldn't* do. She couldn't go home.

Pride and shame. You'd never know they are sisters. They appear so different. Pride puffs out her chest. Shame hangs her head. Pride boasts. Shame hides. Pride seeks to be seen. Shame seeks to go unnoticed.

But don't be fooled, both emotions spring from the same source. And both emotions have the same effect. They keep you from your Father.

Pride says, "You're too good for him."

Shame says, "You're too bad for him."

Pride drives you away.

Shame keeps you away.

If pride is what goes before a fall, then shame is what keeps you from getting up after you fall.

If Madeline knew anything, she knew how to dance. Her father had taught her.

Maybe it wouldn't be so bad, dancing in that club. It's not like I'll have to talk to people or anything. I'll just pretend I'm all alone. And think about something else!

But it was bad. She *hated* the way they all looked at her. But she had no other choices. So Madeline danced as hard as she could. And took the dollars that bought her a place to stay and food to eat. And tried not to think about it.

In fact, she got really good at not thinking about it. Until the letters came.

The cousin brought them, the cousin whose place they'd stayed at when they first came to town. Not one letter, or two, but a box full. All addressed to her. All from her father.

"Sure had trouble tracking *you* down," the cousin complained. "Your old boyfriend must have gone home and squealed on you. These come two or three a week. And I've got better things to do than deliver your mail. Give him your address."

Oh, but she couldn't do that. He might find her.

She couldn't bear to open the envelopes. She knew what they said; he wanted her home. But if he knew what she was doing, he wouldn't.

It seemed less painful not to read them. So she didn't. Not that week, nor the next when the cousin brought more, nor the next when he came again. She kept them in the dressing room at the club, organized according to postmark. She ran her finger over the top of each, but couldn't bring herself to open even one.

She could never go home again. It was better just not to think about it. So she didn't.

In time the leaves fell and the air chilled. The mail came and the cousin complained and the stack of letters grew. Still she refused to send her father an address. And she refused to read a letter. And she danced.

Then a few days before Christmas Eve another letter arrived. Same shape. Same color. But this one had no postmark, or stamp. And it was not delivered by the cousin. It was sitting on her dressing room table.

"A couple of days ago a big man stopped by and asked me to give this to you," explained one of the other dancers. "Said you'd understand the message."

"He was here?" she asked anxiously.

The other girl shrugged. "Suppose he had to be."

Madeline swallowed hard and looked at the envelope. Then she opened it and took out the card. "I know where you are," she read. "I know what you do. That doesn't change the way I feel. What I've said in each letter is still true."

"But I don't know what you've said!" Madeline pulled a letter from the top of the stack and read it. Then a second and a third. Each one ended with the same sentence. Each sentence asked the same question.

In a matter of moments the floor was littered with paper and her face was streaked with tears.

Within an hour she was on a bus. "I just might make it in time."

She barely did.

The relatives were starting to leave. Joe was helping

Grandma in the kitchen when his brother called from the suddenly quiet den. "Joe, someone is here to see you."

Joe stepped out of the kitchen and stopped. In one hand the girl held a backpack. In the other she held a letter. Joe saw the question in her eyes.

"The answer is 'yes,'" she said to her father. "If the invitation is still good, the answer is 'yes.'"

Joe swallowed hard. "Oh, my. The invitation is good."

And so the two of them danced together again on Christmas Eve.

On the floor, near the door, lay a letter with Madeline's name and her father's request.

"Will you come home and dance with your poppa again?"

...the floor was littered with paper and her face was streaked with tears.

All Dressed Up and *Somewhere* to Go!

"I Will Give You My Robe"
(God's Promise in the Garment)

Christ himself died for you.
And that one death paid for your sins.
He was not guilty, but he died for those
who are guilty. He did this to bring
you all to God. His body was killed,
but he was made alive in the spirit.

I PETER 3:18 ICB

But Christ without guilt . . . took upon
himself our punishment, in order that he might thus
expiate our guilt, and do away with our punishment.

AUGUSTINE

Lisa studied the colorful rack of clothing with intent golden eyes. Nice. Very nice. But not exactly what she had in mind. Where was it? She was *sure* she remembered seeing something very special that would be just perfect—there! There it was, shoved way down at the very end. *The* dress! And it was every bit as perfect as she remembered.

And if anyone knew what qualified as perfection in clothing, it was Lisa. She was an expert on the subject. Want to know what's new . . . what's hot . . . what's "in"? Just look at Lisa. Want to know where to find the most fab gear? Just follow Lisa around the mall. If it was the newest . . . the coolest . . . the absolute last word . . . in clothing, Lisa was wearing it!

No one was quite sure how she did it. (She never mentioned all the baby-sitting that took up the dollar gap when she couldn't convince her mom and dad to foot the bill. Masters of illusion never reveal their secrets!)

Even her parents—who knew her very well indeed—were often as bewildered as her friends by the fashionable little "butterfly" they'd hatched.

"My goodness, Lisa," her mother would say, "there *are* more important things in life than clothes, you know!"

Well, of course there are! Lisa knew that. Values. Integrity. The way you treat people. Those were the things that really counted—the things that made you . . . *you!* Everything else was only window dressing. But as long as she had her inside priorities straight, what was the harm in making the *outside* look good, too? Besides, there was just something about knowing she *looked* good that made her *feel* good.

Which was the whole point of *this* "shopping trip." And she'd found exactly what she was looking for! Long, floaty, sprinkled with lavender flowers, it was the dress of any girl's dreams. With a yip of delight, Lisa plucked her find from Jenny Archer's closet.

"Now, wait just a minute, Lisa," Jenny sputtered. "I love that dress!"

"Well, of course, Jenny. That's the whole idea," said Lisa absently, turning the hanger to admire the ripple and flow of the skirt. "Besides, when was the last time you wore it?"

Jenny rolled her eyes. Was Lisa a mind reader, too? It *had* been almost a year since—"That's not the point!" Then she sighed. "Okay, tell me more about this 'good cause' of yours—and what it's got to do with *my* closet."

Lisa looked at her with wide, innocent eyes. "Oh, it's not just *your* closet, Jen," she answered. "I've been in Karen's and Emma's and Molly's and Caitlin's—"

"So, why are you raiding all your friends' closets?" Jenny interrupted.

"You're going to love it, Jen . . ."

Scripture says little about the clothes Jesus wore. We know what his cousin John the Baptist wore. We know what the religious leaders wore. But the clothing of Jesus is unremarkable; neither so humble as to touch hearts nor so glamorous as to turn heads.

One reference to Jesus' garments *is* noteworthy: "They divided his clothes among the four of them. They also took his robe, but it was seamless, woven in one piece from the top. So they said, 'Let's not tear it but throw dice to see who gets it'" (John 19:23–24 NLT).

> Jesus was like his robe: uninterrupted perfection.

It must have been Jesus' finest possession. Jewish tradition called for a mother to make such a robe and present it to her son as a departure gift when he left home. Had Mary done this for Jesus? We don't know. But we do know the tunic was without seam, woven from top to bottom. Why is this important?

Scripture often describes our behavior as the clothes we wear. Peter urges us to be "clothed with humility" (1 Peter 5:5 NKJV). David speaks of evil people who clothe themselves "with cursing" (Psalm 109:18 NKJV). Garments can symbolize character, and like his garment, Jesus' character was seamless. Coordinated. Unified. Jesus was like his robe: uninterrupted perfection.

"Woven . . . from the top." Jesus wasn't led by his own mind; he was led by the mind of his Father. Listen to his words:

"The Son can do nothing alone. The Son does only what he

sees his Father doing. The Son does whatever the Father does" (John 5:19 ICB).

"I can do nothing alone. I judge only the way I am told, so my judgment is right. I don't try to please myself. I try to please the One who sent me" (John 5:30 ICB).

The character of Jesus was a seamless fabric woven from heaven to earth ... from God's thoughts to Jesus' actions. From God's tears to Jesus' compassion. From God's word to Jesus' response. All one piece. All a picture of the character of Jesus.

But when Christ was nailed to the cross, he took off his robe of seamless perfection and slipped into a different wardrobe. The wardrobe of indignity.

The indignity of nakedness. Stripped before his own mother and loved ones. Shamed before his family.

The indignity of failure. For a few pain-filled hours, the religious leaders were the victors, and Christ appeared the loser. Shamed before his accusers.

Worst of all, he wore the *indignity of sin.* "Christ carried our sins in his body on the cross. He did this so that we would stop living for sin and start living for what is right. And we are healed because of his wounds" (1 Peter 2:24 ICB).

The clothing of Christ on the cross? Sin—yours and mine. The sins of all humanity.

I can remember my father explaining to me the reason a group of men on the side of the road wore striped clothing. "They're prisoners," he said. "They have broken the law and are serving time."

You want to know what struck me about those men? They never

looked up. They never made eye contact. Were they ashamed? Probably so.

What they felt on the side of the road was what our Savior felt on the cross—disgrace. Everything about the crucifixion was intended not only to hurt the victim, but to shame him.

Death on a cross was usually reserved for the most vile offenders: slaves, murderers, assassins, and the like. The condemned person was marched through the city streets, shouldering his crossbar and wearing a sign around his neck that named his crime. At the execution site he was stripped and mocked.

Jenny smiled to herself as her bubbly little friend started to explain her project—in her usual breathless, rambling style. She'd always suspected there was a lot more to Lisa than a dazzling smile, amusing chatter . . . and a fantastic wardrobe. But this . . . ?

"It was really my cousin Nicole's idea," said Lisa, unfolding her story in fits and starts. "Well, maybe not exactly *her* idea . . . more like an inspiration . . . something actually that her mom was doing that sort of—. You know Nicole, don't you, Jen? My cousin who—"

"—your cousin who lives across town and goes to Arts Magnet School. The dancer," finished Jenny with a laugh. "Sure, I know her. Now take a breath, Lisa, and start over. I'm still a little confused. As if you didn't know."

"Okay, you know how it is when you're getting dressed up for some really special occasion . . . and you have just the absolutely perfect thing to wear? How *good* it feels—how special *you* feel—to know you look your very best?" asked Lisa.

Jenny nodded. "Sure, it's a great feeling," she agreed, with a pointed look at the dress with the lavender flowers.

But Lisa refused to be distracted. "Okay, now think how it would be to *never* have that feeling. Never have one wonderful dress that made you feel . . . special." Lisa's golden eyes grew very serious. "You know, Jen, there are a lot of girls—girls just like us—who never *do* get to have that feeling. Everything they have is either a hand-me-down or comes from a thrift shop. Imagine wearing something like that to your own graduation!"

> "*. . . Imagine wearing something like that to your own graduation!*"

Jenny *could* imagine it. And what she thought was written all over her face.

Lisa knew she had her! "But what if . . . what *if*, Jen, there was a place those girls could go—a special "closet"—filled with wonderful things to choose from?! Not tatty old things someone else was tired of, but really cool, up-to-date clothes any girl would be proud to wear?"

Jenny nodded, right on cue. "Well . . . there *is!*" finished Lisa triumphantly. "All we have to do is fill it. Well, actually . . .

fill *them*. Before graduation time." And the rest of the story came tumbling out.

The project was born when Lisa and her cousin heard about something that Nicole's lawyer mom and her friends were involved with. Each of them was donating one of her best business outfits to a Career Closet for women in job-training programs. "So they could look really *fine* for job interviews. Well, Nicole and I saw the possibilities right away—"

"Well, of *course* you did," Jenny teased.

Lisa grinned back. "So Nicole talked to the youth group at *her* church. And I talked to mine. And one of those girls had a friend at another school . . . Anyway, everyone loves the idea. And here's the best part, Jen—"

Lisa stopped for just a quick breath, and Jenny grabbed the opportunity. "How could there be a 'best' part?" she asked with a smile. "The whole thing sounds pretty terrific to me."

Lisa beamed. "Oh, it gets even better," she assured her. "Each church group is collecting from kids they know in their area. Then we swap our collections—fill the 'closets' at each *other's* churches! See?"

Jenny *did* see. Each church and school was in a different part of town. So no girl who got one of the gift dresses had to worry about being embarrassed. The chances of the girl wearing the dress and the girl who donated it being at the same graduation or party were practically zilch. And the church staffs would know which girls to invite—very quietly—to choose a dress. It *was* a stroke of genius!

"Brilliant, Lisa. Just brilliant." Jenny applauded. Then she frowned. "But you know, I'm not so sure I can let those lavender flowers go—" Lisa's face fell. "—all by themselves. They've really grown very attached to that yellow one of mine."

For once, Lisa was speechless. Almost. "The yellow *silk?* But that's . . . that's your very favorite dress of all time!"

"Yes, it is," Jenny agreed with a rueful smile. "I suppose that's why they call it a . . . 'sacrifice.'"

Lisa just stared as Jenny reached into her closet for the shimmer of yellow silk. Then she smiled and hugged her friend. "Oh, no, Jen. That's why they call it . . . *love.*"

When Jesus was nailed to the cross to die a criminal's death, he was shamed before everyone who was there watching. But that wasn't the worst part. This was: Jesus was not only shamed before people, he was shamed before heaven.

Since he bore the sin of the murderer and the thief, he felt the shame of the murderer and thief. Though he never lied, he bore the disgrace of a liar. Though he never cheated, he felt the embarrassment of a cheater. Since he bore the sin of the world, he felt the collective shame of the world.

It's no wonder that the Hebrew writer spoke of the "disgrace he bore" (Hebrews 13:13 NLT).

While on the cross, Jesus felt the indignity and disgrace of a criminal. No, he was not guilty. No, he had not committed a sin. And, no, he did not deserve to be sentenced. But you and I were, we had, and we did. We were clothed in garments of sin and shame. But Jesus took them from us at the cross. Indeed, he did much more than that. With infinite love and generosity, he offers us a robe of seamless purity and puts on our patchwork coats of pride, greed, and selfishness. "He changed places with us" (Galatians 3:13). He wore our sin so we could wear his righteousness.

Though we come to the cross dressed in sin, we leave the cross dressed in the "coat of his strong love" (Isaiah 59:17), wrapped with a belt of "goodness and fairness" (Isaiah 11:5), and clothed in "garments of salvation" (Isaiah 61:10 NIV).

Indeed, we leave dressed in Christ himself. "You have all put on Christ as a garment" (Galatians 3:27 NEB).

It wasn't enough for him to prepare you a feast.

It wasn't enough for him to reserve you a seat.

It wasn't enough for him to cover the cost and provide the transportation to the banquet.

He did something more. He let you wear his own clothes so that you could be properly dressed.

He did that . . . just for you.

Jenny smiled as she watched Lisa flit down the front walk, carrying the yellow silk and lavender-flowered dresses in careful hands.

I'm going to miss that yellow dress. But, hey, it's going somewhere really special—

Come to think of it, there was one thing she still didn't know. "Hey, Lisa, you never did say. What are you and Nicole calling this whole thing?"

Lisa spun around and beamed a delighted smile back at Jenny. "Oh, coming up with a name was the *easy* part. What else could we call it but . . .
My Friend's Closet?"

Anyone Can *Talk* a Good Game; But It's How You Play It That Counts!

"I Understand Your Pain" *(God's Promise in the Wine-Soaked Sponge)*

For our high priest [Jesus] is able to understand our weaknesses. When he lived on earth, he was tempted in every way that we are, but he did not sin.

HEBREWS 4:15 ICB

Jesus wept.

JOHN 11:35 NIV

Trust

Ever tried to convince a mouse not to worry? Ever succeeded in pacifying the panic of a rodent? If so, you are wiser than I. My attempt was not successful. My comforting words fell on tiny, deaf ears.

Not that the fellow deserved any kindness, mind you. Because of him, Denalyn screamed. Because of the scream, the garage shook. Because the garage shook, I was yanked out of dreamland and off my La-Z-Boy and called to defend my wife and country. I was proud to go. Head high, shoulders back, I marched into the garage.

The mouse never had a chance. I know jujitsu, karate, tae kwan do, and several other . . . uh, phrases. I've even watched self-defense infomercials. This mouse had met his match.

Besides, he was trapped in an empty trash can. How he got there, only he knows, and he ain't telling. I know, I asked him. His only reply was a mad dash around the base of the can.

The poor guy was scared to the tip of his whiskers. And who wouldn't be? Imagine being caged in a plastic container and looking up only to see the large (though handsome) face of a human. Would be enough to make you chuck up your cheese.

"What are you going to do with him?" Denalyn asked, clutching my arm for courage.

"Don't worry, little darlin'," I replied. "I'll go easy on the little fellow."

So off we went—the mouse, the trash can, and me, marching down the cul-de-sac toward an empty lot. "Stick with me, little guy. I'll have you home in no time." He didn't listen. You'd have thought we were walking to death row. Had I not placed a lid on the can, the furry fellow would have jumped out. "I'm not going to hurt you," I explained. "I'm going to free you. You got yourself into a mess; I'm going to get you out."

He never calmed down. He never sat still. He never—well, he never trusted me. Even at the last moment, when I tilted the can on the ground and set him free, did he turn around and say thank you? Did he invite me to his mouse house for a meal? No. He just ran (Was it my imagination, or did I hear him shouting, "Get back! Get back! Max, the mouse-hater, is here"?)

Honestly. What would I have to do to win his trust? Learn to speak Mouse-agese? Grow beady eyes and a long tail? Get down in the trash with him? Thanks, but no thanks. I mean, the mouse was cute and all, but he wasn't worth that much.

Apparently, you and I are.

Did he invite me to his mouse house for a meal?

You think it's absurd for a man to become a mouse? The journey from your house to a trash can is far shorter than the one from heaven to earth. But Jesus took it. Why?

He wants us to trust him.

Let's take a closer look at that thought for a moment. Why did Jesus live on earth as long as he did? Couldn't his life have been much shorter? Why not step into our world just long enough to die for our sins and then leave? Why not a sinless year or week? Why did he have to live a life? To take on our sins is one thing, but to take on our sunburns, our sore throats? To experience death, yes—but to put up with life? To put up with long roads, long days, and short tempers. Why did he do it?

This time he'd really done it! Messed up *big* time.

Kyle was in major trouble, and he knew it. All thanks to those Famous Last Words of his—words he could never seem to resist using: "No problemo. Trust me, guys."

He should have known better. It wasn't as if his dad hadn't warned him about it often enough.

"Look, son, having confidence in yourself is great. But there's a lot more to it than just *talking* a good game. You have to back up what you *say* with what you *do*. Coming up with exciting ideas is a fine thing. But you'd better be able to deliver on those promises, or you'll be losing friends faster than even *you* can make them.

"Trust is very important in any relationship. In fact, without it, you won't even *have* a relationship. And saying 'trust me' is *not* enough. You have to prove that you're *worthy* of trust."

But had he listened? Now, thanks entirely to him, the class project for the science fair was a total disaster! What *had* he been thinking?!

Which was the whole problem. He hadn't been thinking. Just shooting off his mouth. Planning to work out the details later. Trying to make a good impression on the popular kids at school.

To make it even worse, the idea they already *had* was pretty cool. But, as he usually did, Kyle saw a way to make it even snazzier. And his enthusiasm, as it usually did, carried everyone else right along with him. Everyone, except Stacy.

"Are you sure, Kyle?" she asked. "That's going to take some pretty complicated wiring. And if we change it to include that, there won't be time to change it back. Are you sure you can do it . . . ?"

Well, of course he was sure. Kyle was always sure. Never mind that he had never actually done anything that tricky. How hard could it be?! A couple of books from the library, a little reading . . . piece of cake! Or so he thought. Right up until he threw the switch for a test run. And blew the project . . . the main electrical circuit for the entire school . . . and the confidence of his team.

Trust is a very fragile thing. Difficult to win. Easy to lose. Not something we can simply ask for. It must be earned—not by what we say, but by what we *do*. Jesus knew that. And throughout every moment of his life—and in every detail of his death—he worked tirelessly to earn our trust. Even his final act on earth was intended to prove he was worthy of that trust.

Later, knowing that all was now completed, and so that the Scripture would be fulfilled, Jesus said, "I am thirsty." A jar of wine vinegar was there, so they soaked a sponge in it, put the sponge on a stalk of the hyssop plant, and lifted it to Jesus' lips. When he had received the drink, Jesus said, "It is finished." With that, he bowed his head and gave up his spirit. (John 19:28–30 NIV)

This is the final act of Jesus' life. In his last moments of earthly life, we hear the sounds of a thirsty man.

And through his thirst—through a sponge and a jar of sour wine vinegar—he tells us again:

"You can trust me."

Jesus. Lips cracked and mouth of cotton. Throat so dry he couldn't swallow, and voice so hoarse he could scarcely speak. He is thirsty. To find the last time moisture touched those lips you need to rewind a dozen hours to the meal in the Upper Room. Since tasting that cup of wine at the Last Supper, Jesus has been beaten, spit upon, bruised, and cut. He has been a cross-carrier and sin-bearer, and no liquid has soothed his throat. He is thirsty.

Trust is a very fragile thing. Difficult to win. Easy to lose.

Why doesn't he do something about it? Couldn't he? Did he not cause jugs of water to become jugs of wine? Did he not make a wall out of the Jordan River and two walls out of the Red Sea? Didn't he, with one word, banish the rain and calm the waves?

Did God not say, "I will pour water on him who is thirsty" (Isaiah 44:3 NKJV)?

If so, why does Jesus who *is* God suffer thirst?

And while we are asking this question, add a few more. Why did he grow weary in Samaria (John 4:6), disturbed in Nazareth (Mark 6:6), and angry in the Temple (John 2:15)? Why was he sleepy in the boat on the Sea of Galilee (Mark 4:38), sad at the tomb of Lazarus (John 11:35), and hungry in the wilderness (Matthew 4:2)?

And why—*why*—was he thirsty on the cross?

He didn't have to suffer thirst. At least, not to the level he did. Six hours earlier he'd been offered drink, but he refused it.

> They brought Jesus to the place called Golgotha (which means The Place of the Skull). Then they offered him wine mixed with myrrh, but he did not take it. And they crucified him. (Mark 15:22–24 NIV)

Before the nail was pounded, a drink was offered. Wine with myrrh—to numb his senses and soften the pain. But Jesus refused it. He refused to be stupefied by the drug, choosing instead to feel the full force of his suffering.

Why? Why did he leave himself open to all these feelings?

Because he knew you would feel them, too.

Kyle felt awful. No . . . *worse* than awful. He'd been so sure . . .

It really *was* a terrific idea. Who'd have thought that a minor little detail like "practical experience" would make such a difference? Certainly not Kyle.

Which was too bad. Especially now. Four days before the science fair. Looking at the charred wiring of the doomed project—and the faces of his team.

"Thanks a *lot*, man!" said Greg.

"You don't have a clue how to make this work, do you?" added Annie.

And Stacy? Well, *her* eyes were spitting more sparks than his wiring had. "Really, Kyle . . . *we* could have messed up on our own! But, no, we had to go trust some big . . . *expert!*"

And what was there to say to that? Especially when you felt lower than a . . . a worm.

Jesus shared all the feelings he knew you would have. He knew you would be weary, worried, and angry. He knew you'd be sleepy, sad, and hungry. He knew you'd face pain. If not pain of the body, the pain of the soul . . . pain too sharp for any drug. He knew you'd face thirst. If not a thirst for water, at least a thirst for truth. And the truth we learn from the image of a thirsty Christ is this: He understands.

Jesus understands. He's "been there." He's "done that." And because he understands, we can come to him.

In fact, if he *didn't* understand, wouldn't that keep us from him? Doesn't our lack of understanding keep us from others? Suppose you just can't figure out how to stretch your allowance. You need some guidance from a sympathetic friend. Would you go to the son of a zillionaire? Probably not. Why? He would not understand. He's likely never been where you are, so he can't relate to how you feel.

Jesus, however, has and can. He has been where you are and can relate to how you feel. And if his life on earth doesn't convince you, his death on the cross should. He understands what you are going through. Our Lord does not look down on our weaknesses or scoff at our needs. He responds "generously to all without finding fault" (James 1:5 NIV). How can he do this? No one put it more clearly than did the author of Hebrews.

> Jesus understands every weakness of ours, because he was tempted in every way that we are. But he did not sin! So whenever we are in need, we should come bravely before the throne of our merciful God. There we will be treated with undeserved kindness, and we will find help.
> (Hebrews 4:15–16 CEV)

"Wow," said his dad when he heard the details. "*All* the wiring?"

"Every bit," said Kyle, "fried . . . totaled . . . kaput!" He shook his head. "Don't know *what* happened."

"Don't you?" asked his father, lifting one eyebrow.

Kyle studied the toes of his shoes. He did know, of course. He'd gotten carried away again . . . all "promise" and *no* performance. But though his dad may have been thinking *I told you so*, he didn't say it. He never did. Kyle heaved a sigh of relief.

"So," came the next question, "what're you going to do about it?"

Do?! There's nothing to *do*. Kyle shrugged. "Well, I said I was sorry. But they weren't very impressed."

"Can't say that I blame 'em," said his dad. "'Sorry' is a good *beginning*, Kyle. But there's something even better that should come next, remember? 'Let me make—'"

"'—make things right!'" Kyle finished with him. "But how, Dad? This whole wiring thing is a lot harder than I thought. I don't know enough!"

His father handed him the phone. "Then I suggest you put that busy brain to work and find someone who *does*."

It took Kyle two days, and twenty-seven phone calls, but he did find someone. A friend of his dad's, John Wilcox, an electrical engineer. Who—oddly enough—didn't sound all that surprised to hear from Kyle. Who could, indeed, show Kyle how to solve his problem. And who—as it turned out—had an absolutely huge garage that needed cleaning out.

"Ever cleaned a garage, Kyle?" asked Mr. Wilcox.

"Hey, no problemo. **Trus**—Well, actually, I haven't. But I can learn. Experience is a great teacher . . ."

Why did Jesus allow himself to experience thirst? So we would know that he understands; so all who struggle would hear his invitation: "You can trust me."

The word *trust* does not appear in the passage about the wine and sponge, but we do find a phrase that makes it easier to trust. Look at the sentence before the declaration of thirst: "So that the Scripture would be fulfilled, Jesus said, 'I am thirsty'" (John 19:28 NIV). In that verse John gives us the motive behind Jesus' words. Our Lord was concerned about the fulfillment of Scripture. In fact, the fulfillment of Scripture is an ongoing theme in his passion and death. Consider this list:

> The betrayal of Jesus by Judas occurred "to bring about what the Scripture said." (John 13:18; see also John 17:12)

> The gamble for the clothing took place "so that this Scripture would come true: 'They divided my clothes among them, and they threw lots for my clothing.'" (John 19:24)

> The legs of Christ were left unbroken "to make the Scripture come true: 'Not one of his bones will be broken.'" (John 19:36)

The side of Jesus was pierced to fulfill the passage that says, "They will look at the one they stabbed." (John 19:37)

John says the disciples were stunned by the empty tomb since "they did not yet understand from the Scriptures that Jesus must rise from the dead." (John 20:9)

Why so many references to Scripture? Why, in his final moments, was Jesus so determined to fulfill prophecy? Because he knew we would doubt. He knew we would question. And since he did not want our heads to close our *hearts* to his love, he used his final moments to offer proof that he was the Messiah—the One whose coming had been foretold through centuries of prophecy.

...he did not want our heads to close our hearts to his love,...

Every important detail of Jesus' suffering and death had been written down long before:

- *the betrayal by a familiar friend (Psalm 41:9)*
- *the forsaking by the disciples after being offended at him (Psalm 31:11)*
- *the false accusation (Psalm 35:11)*
- *the silence before his judges (Isaiah 53:7)*
- *being proved guiltless (Isaiah 53:9)*
- *being included with sinners (Isaiah 53:12)*

- *being crucified (Psalm 22:16)*
- *the mockery of the spectators (Psalm 109:25)*
- *the taunt of no deliverance (Psalm 22:7–8)*
- *the gambling for his garments (Psalm 22:18)*
- *the prayer for his enemies (Isaiah 53:12)*
- *being forsaken by God (Psalm 22:1)*
- *the yielding of his spirit into the hands of his Father (Psalm 31:5)*
- *the bones not broken (Psalm 34:20)*
- *the burial in a rich man's tomb (Isaiah 53:9)*

In fact, Bible scholars tell us that during his life Jesus fulfilled **332** distinct prophecies in the Old Testament!

Jesus hung on the cross, and said, "I am thirsty." And in those words he gave us one final reminder—one more proof, in a life filled with them—that he is who he says he is: the Messiah. The Son of God. The One we can trust absolutely above all others.

Jesus knows we need someone to trust. Someone who is bigger, stronger, wiser than we are. Someone who loves us absolutely. Someone who understands us perfectly—because he has *been* us.

And in his final message—delivered through a wine-soaked sponge—he tells us this: I am that person. Trust me.

Jesus knows we need someone to trust.

10

C'mon In . . . the Door's Always Open!

"I Invite You into My Presence"
(God's Promise Through the Torn Flesh)

*We can enter through a new way
that Jesus opened for us. It is a living way.
It leads through the curtain—Christ's body.*

HEBREWS 10:20 ICB

*Yes, through Christ we all have the right
to come to the Father in one Spirit.*

EPHESIANS 2:18 ICB

*Let us, then, feel free to come before God's throne.
Here there is grace. And we can receive mercy and
grace to help us when we need it.*

HEBREWS 4:16 ICB

Nicole Ryan stood very still, looking at the battered metal door. She reached out a slender hand and gently stroked the peeling green paint, remembering *another* door. A door of shining, polished golden oak. A door she'd slammed shut, in tears, last February—leaving everything she'd dreamed of, everything she'd worked so hard for, on the other side. Out of her reach forever.

Madame Nevetsky's words had made that perfectly clear.

Months later, Nicole could still remember how confused and hurt she'd been that February day. She could still hear the angry thoughts that had raced through her head: *It's not fair. It's not! What was God thinking?! To give me such a wonderful gift, then fix things so I can't use it?*

But that was exactly what had happened. The dream was over. The door was closed.

Or so it seemed . . . that February day to Nicole.

Imagine a person standing in front of the White House. Better still, imagine *yourself* standing in front of the White House.

That's you on the sidewalk, peering through the fence, over the lawn, at the home of the president. That's you—in fine form—hair in place and shoes shined. That's you turning toward the entrance. Your pace is brisk and stride sure. It should be. You have come to meet with the president.

You have a few matters you wish to discuss with him.

First, there is the matter of the fire hydrant in front of your house. Could they soften the red just a shade? It's too bright.

Then there's the issue of world peace. You are for it—would he create it?

And last, college tuition is way too high—your parents will never be able to afford it. Could he call that college you dream of and ask them to lighten up?

All worthy issues, right? Won't take more than a few minutes. Besides, you brought him some cookies he can share with the first lady and the first puppy. So with bag in hand and a smile on your face, you step up to the gate and announce to the guard, "I'd like to see the president, please."

He asks for your name, and you give it. He looks at you and then at his list and says, "We have no record of your appointment."

"You have to have an appointment?"

"Yes."

"How do I get one?"

"Through his office staff."

"Could I have their number?"

"No, it's restricted."

"Then how can I get in?"

"It's better to wait until they call you."

"But they don't know me!"

The guard shrugs. "Then they probably won't call."

And so you sigh and turn and begin your trip home. Your questions are unanswered and your needs unmet.

And you were so close! Had the president stepped out onto the lawn, you could've waved, and he would've waved back. You were only yards from his front door . . . but you might as well have been miles. The two of you were separated by the fence and the guard.

Then there was the problem of the Secret Service. Had you somehow entered, they would have stopped you. The staff would have done the same. There were too many barriers.

And what about the invisible barriers? Barriers of time. (The president's too busy.) Barriers of status. (You're not important enough.) Barriers of protocol. (You have to go through the right channels.) You leave the White House with nothing more than a hard lesson learned. You do not have access to the president. Your chat with the commander in chief? It ain't gonna happen. You'll have to take your problem about peace and your question about the cost of college with you. There are too many barriers. The door is closed.

Nicole wasn't at all used to closed doors. Her talent— her special *gift*—had been opening doors for her all her life.

Nicole was a dancer—a very gifted dancer—who had always known that someday she would be a prima ballerina. And she wasn't the only one who thought so. Her first dance teachers had seen, and nurtured, her rare talent. Her own hard work had earned her a coveted place in the Arts Magnet School. And, at fourteen, she was already known as a budding star of the City Ballet Company.

Nicole wasn't just a girl who danced. Dance was *who* she was. Everyone who knew her knew that. And agreed. To them she was never just "Nicole," but always "Nicole the Dancer." It just felt . . . right. As "right" as the brilliant future in ballet everyone predicted for her.

Then, last February, everything changed.

Madame Irina Nevetsky's usually stern face was kind, as she took Nicole aside after practice. That alone made Nicole just a little nervous.

The company ballet mistress generally wore only one expression: critical. Her piercing eyes saw every flaw, caught every break in form, noted the slightest fall from grace. Her favorite words were: "You can do better."

Praise from Madame Nevetsky was rare—though Nicole had earned more than her share. A look of kindness and concern, unheard of. And to see those stern eyes filled with . . . what? Regret?! . . . positively unnerving.

"I'm sorry, Nicole, but we can no longer ignore reality. Over the past months you've simply grown too tall."

Nicole hung her head. (Which didn't make her the least bit shorter.) She'd tried very hard to ignore her astonishing spurt of growth. Three inches this year! Three inches added to her former five feet, seven inches. Three inches that a fashion model would consider a blessing. Three inches that a basketball player would welcome with glee. But for a classical dancer? Three inches that were nothing less than a . . . disaster!

"What are you now, Nicole," Madame Nevetsky asked gently, "five-foot-ten?" Nicole nodded miserably. "And, of course, in toe shoes, en pointe, you'll be even taller. Over six feet, and at fourteen you're still growing," Madame Nevetsky went on.

"I think you know—indeed, my dear, you *must* know—that no major ballet company has a place for a girl that tall. It's simply too difficult to find a male dancer to partner you."

Nicole did know. But that didn't make the pain of her shattered dream any less sharp. *How could God let this happen?!*

Tears filled Nicole's eyes as the ballet mistress placed a gentle hand on hers. "I know, my dear, it hurts. Classical ballet is closed to you. But your gift for dance remains as rare and beautiful as it has always been. And there are many other ways you can—"

But Nicole wasn't interested in "other ways." *It's so unfair!* Eyes filled with angry tears, she'd jerked her hand away, turned, and ran out the door, slamming it behind her. Closed!

Yes, some doors are pretty firmly closed. And—like Nicole Ryan's future in ballet—your chances of wandering in off the street at the White House and seeing the president *are* pretty bleak. Unless . . . unless, that is, *he* takes the initiative. Unless he, spotting you on the sidewalk, takes pity on your plight and says to his chief of staff, "See that person with the bag of cookies? Go tell him I'd like to talk with him for a minute."

If he gives such a command, all the barriers will drop. The Oval Office will call the head of security. The head of security will call the guard, and the guard will call your name. "Guess what? I can't explain it, but the door to the Oval Office is wide open."

You stop and turn and straighten your shoulders and enter the same door where—only moments before—you were shut out. The guard is the same. The gates are the same. The security people are the same. But the situation is not the same. You can now go where before you could not.

And, what's more, *you* are not the same. You feel special, chosen. Why? Because the man up there saw you down here and made it possible for you to come in.

Okay, you're right. It *is* a fanciful story. Could never happen. You and I both know when it comes to the president, don't hold your breath—no invitation will arrive. But when it comes to God? Well, pick up your cookies and walk in—because it already *has* happened!

He has spotted you. He has heard you and has invited you. What once separated you has been removed: "Now in Christ Jesus, you who were far away from God are brought near" (Ephesians 2:13). Nothing remains between you and God but an open door.

> Nothing remains between you and God but an open door.

But how could this be? If we can't get in to see the president, how could we be granted an audience with God? What happened? In a word, someone removed the curtain. Someone tore down the veil. Someone opened the door.

The door to Nicole's room stayed closed quite a lot that February and March. She didn't want to see anyone. She didn't want to talk to anyone—though (amazingly!) Madame Nevetsky had called several times. Nicole just wanted to be alone.

She spent long hours shut in her room during those weeks. Hurt. Confused. Angry. Very angry—especially with God! (He was used to that.) She needed to understand. She needed *someone* to blame. (God was used to *that*, too.)

But no one can stay angry forever. Especially when God—and Madame Nevetsky—take a hand.

"All right, my dear, I know you're hurting," said the persistent ballet mistress when Nicole finally came to the phone. "But really, Nicole, you can do better than this!"

Do better? How? There's nothing to do!

But there was, of course. And Madame Nevetsky was prepared to list it all.

"There's more to dance than just our beloved ballet, you know. Many other ways to use this wonderful gift of yours. There are fine modern dance companies where height doesn't matter. There's choreography . . . teaching . . . so many ways to use your talent. But that's not what I called about . . ."

And, indeed, it wasn't. What she had in mind for Nicole at the moment was something quite different. "You were very fortunate, Nicole. Your gift was recognized and trained. Every door was open to you. But God gives gifts in other places, too. To children who live in a world of *closed* doors. Children without your advantages. Children whose talents may never be noticed or encouraged. Unless *someone* goes looking.

"Let me tell you about something special we're doing this summer at an inner-city community center. A door *you* can help open . . ."

Something very special happened at the cross—something beyond wondrous occurred in the death of Christ—that opened a door for you and me. And that something is described by the writer of Hebrews.

> So, brothers and sisters, we are completely free to enter the
> Most Holy Place without fear because of the blood of Jesus'
> death. We can enter through a new and living way that Jesus
> opened for us. It leads through the curtain—Christ's body.
> (Hebrews 10:19–20)

To the original readers of that letter, those last four words were explosive: "the curtain—Christ's body." According to the writer, the curtain equaled Jesus! Hence, whatever happened to the flesh of Jesus happened to the curtain between us and God. What happened to his flesh? It was torn. Torn by the whips, torn by the thorns. Torn by the weight of the cross and the points of the nails. But in the horror of his torn flesh, we find the splendor of the open door.

"But Jesus cried out again in a loud voice and died. Then the curtain in the Temple was torn into two pieces, from the top to the bottom" (Matthew 27:50–51).

The curtain is nothing short of the curtain of the Temple. The veil that hung before the Holy of Holies.

The Holy of Holies, you'll remember, was a part of the Temple no one could enter. Jewish worshipers could enter the outer court, but only the priests could enter the Holy Place. And no one, except the high priest on one day a year, entered the Holy of Holies. No one. Why? Because the "shekinah glory"—the glory of God—was present there.

If you were told you were free to enter the Oval Office of the White House, you'd probably shake your head and chuckle. "You're one brick short of a load, buddy." Multiply your disbelief by a thousand, and you'll have an idea how a Jew would feel if someone told him he could enter the Holy of Holies. "Yeah, right. You're one bagel short of a dozen."

No one but the high priest entered the Holy of Holies. *No one.* In no uncertain terms, the curtain declared: "This far and no farther!"

What did fifteen hundred years of a curtain-draped Holy of Holies communicate? Simple. God is holy ... separate from us, not to be approached. Even Moses was told, "You cannot see my face. No one can see me and stay alive" (Exodus 33:20 ICB). God is holy, and we are sinners, and there is a distance between us.

Isn't this our problem? We know God is good. We know we are not, and we feel far from God. The ancient words of Job are ours: "I wish there was someone to make peace between us" (Job 9:33 ICB).

Oh, but there is! Jesus hasn't left us with an unapproachable God. Yes, God is holy. Yes, we are sinful. But, yes, yes, yes, Jesus is our mediator—the One who "goes between" us and God. "There is only one God. And there is only one way that people can reach God. That way is through Jesus Christ, who is also a man" (1 Timothy 2:5 ICB). Jesus was the curtain between us and God. And his flesh was torn!

What appeared to be the cruelty of man was actually the mercy of God. Matthew tells us, "And when Jesus had cried out again in a loud voice, he gave up his spirit. *At that moment* the curtain of the temple was torn in two from top to bottom" (Matthew 27:50–51 NIV, italics mine).

It's as if the hands of heaven had been gripping the veil, waiting for this moment. One instant it was whole; the next it was ripped in two from top to bottom. No delay. No hesitation.

What did the torn curtain mean? For the Jews it meant no more barrier between them and the Holy of Holies. No more priests to go between them and God. No more animal sacrifices to atone for their sins.

And for us? What did the torn curtain mean for us? Everything.

Because of what happened at the cross, because the curtain was torn, we are welcome to enter into God's presence—any day, any time. God has removed the barrier that separates us from him. The barrier of sin that rose up between us and our Father in Eden's garden is down. Gone. God has already dealt with our mistakes at the cross.

He has removed the curtain. The door is open, and God invites us in. We are welcome. And we don't even have to bring cookies.

On a beautiful June afternoon—*ages* away from the pain of February—Nicole Ryan stood at the battered metal door of the shabby inner-city community center. Smiling.

Madame Nevetsky had been right. There *were* many kinds of dance. And many *ways* for a dancer to practice her art, and honor her gift. In fact, just last week a touring Irish dance company had captured her heart with their lilting music and flowing grace. Definitely worth looking into. But that was for later.

Madame had been right about something else, too: Every time one door closes, another opens!

Nicole reached out a slender hand, opened *this* unexpected door, and stepped through. And came face-to-face with . . . joy!

Lined up in a not-too-tidy row, beaming back at her, stood fifteen little girls. White faces. Black faces. Brown and golden faces. A *rainbow* of little girls. Little girls in patched tights, sagging leotards, and scuffed, borrowed ballet shoes. Little girls, with eyes bright as stars, who practically *vibrated* with excitement. Because today—today!—*they* were going to learn to dance!

Every time one door closes, another opens!

The Gift That Keeps On Giving

"I Have Redeemed You and I Will Keep You"
(God's Promise in the Blood and Water)

*But Christ offered one sacrifice for sins,
and it is good forever. Then he sat down at the right
side of God. . . . With one sacrifice he made perfect
forever those who are being made holy.*

HEBREWS 10:12, 14 ICB

*True love is God's love for us,
not our love for God. God sent his Son
to be the way to take away our sins.*

1 JOHN 4:10 ICB

Ever played a team sport? Pretty exciting stuff, right? Especially when your team wins. Of course, even when your team doesn't win there are still a lot of good things going on for you. Exercise. Excitement. Energy—that little extra "zing" that comes with being part of something bigger than yourself. All that happens, win *or* lose.

But when your team *does* win? Ah, that's when things get *really* interesting—when something very special happens. And you don't even have to be the best player on the team. In fact, you can be the very worst player on the team, and it still happens as much for you as it does for the team star. When your team wins, *you* are a winner, too! You share in the credit for the good work of someone else simply by being on the team.

Hasn't Jesus done the same for you? If you've accepted Jesus as your Savior, haven't you taken a place on God's team?

What your sports team does for you on game day, your Lord does for you *every* day. Because of his performance, you cross the finish line of each day with a perfect score. Doesn't matter if you goofed "here" or messed up "there." What matters is that you showed up to play and joined the right team. In this case, an unbeatable team: you, the Father, the Son, and the Holy Spirit. A better team doesn't exist.

You are given the prize, not because of what you do, but because of whom you know—the team you are on.

Pretty cool, right? But there's something even cooler going on with you and God. It's the *other* thing that happens when you play on a team. Something that takes place *inside* you.

Think about it. Haven't you ever noticed how playing on a team—especially a team with better players than you are—makes *you* play better, too? As the game progresses you find yourself moving a little more smoothly . . . digging a little deeper . . . playing a little harder . . . to live up to the quality of your team. In short, because of being on the team, you *change*.

Where am I headed with all this? Here's where:

- *Simply by being on a winning team, you are a winner, too. That's what it does **for** you.*

- *Because of playing on the team, you become a better player. That's what happens **in** you.*

- *When Jesus died on the cross for our sins, we were saved. That's Christ's work **for** us.*

- *Because of Jesus' death on the cross, we can become a little better . . . a little stronger in spirit . . . a little holier . . . every day. That's Christ's work **in** us.*

Christ's work for us.

Christ's work in us.

Both are gifts of God.

"With one sacrifice he made perfect forever those who are being made holy" (Hebrews 10:14). See the two tenses: past and present? We *were* "made perfect." A done deal. We *are* "being made holy." Still happening. Every day.

Jesus spread his arms wide to die on the cross. Has there ever been a more perfect—more *loving*—relationship?"

Lauren plucked at the filmy skirt of her long gown and frowned into the mirror. Then she spun around and looked back over her shoulder to check out the puffy bow and long streamers of the wide satin sash. *A sash, for heaven's sake!* The back view didn't please her any more than the front did.

It's all so juvenile! And so . . . pink. Then her lips twitched, then the twitch became a smile. *Why am I surprised? Pink is the bride's favorite color.*

When she thought about the bride—and the groom—the smile became a chuckle, and her eyes were warm with love.

This whole wedding was *so* like them. Kind of wacky. And very, very sweet. And if they wanted a thirteen-year-old flower girl—in a *very* pink dress—that's what they'd get. Along with a six-foot-tall ring bearer. Lauren laughed right out loud when she remembered the look on her fifteen-year-old brother's face when he got *that* bit of news.

Lauren took another look in the mirror. Nope. The dress hadn't improved in the slightest. *Oh, well, just think of it as another wedding gift.* Families! What are you going to do?!

Relationships are strange and wonderful things. And none more so than our relationship with God. And the gifts he gives—the work he does *for* us, and *in* us.

God's work for us. God's work in us. Two beautiful, *powerful* gifts. Neglect the first, and you grow fearful. Neglect the second, and you grow lazy. Either would be a shame, because these gifts were given at the cross. Indeed, signs of both can be seen in the moistened dirt at the foot of the cross. Let's take a closer look at the first:

God's work for us.

Listen to this passage: "But one of the soldiers stuck his spear into Jesus' side, and at once blood and water came out" (John 19:34). In Scripture, there has always been a connection between blood and mercy. As far back as Abel, one of the first sons of Adam, worshipers knew that "without the shedding of blood there is no forgiveness" (Hebrews 9:22 NIV).

How Abel, a simple shepherd, knew this truth is anyone's guess, but somehow he knew to offer more than prayers and crops. He knew to offer a life. He knew to pour out more than his heart and his desires; he knew to pour out blood. With a field as his temple and the ground as his altar, Abel chose the finest sheep in his flock and became the first to do what millions would imitate. He offered a blood sacrifice for sins. And God was very pleased with Abel and his gift.

But for Abel's brother, Cain, the story was quite different. Cain, too, brought a gift to God. But he chose to offer only food from his fields. And when his gift was rejected by God, Cain was so angry and hurt and jealous of Abel that he murdered his brother!

Abel and Cain. Two brothers. One chose what was pleasing to God. One did not. And the consequences were *enormous*.

In those days, in those times, it was blood that was required. And those who followed Abel's example form a long line: Abraham, Moses, Gideon, Samson, Saul, David, Jacob, Aaron . . . They knew the shedding of blood was necessary for the forgiveness of sins.

But the line ended at the cross. What Abel sought to accomplish in the field, God achieved with his Son. What Abel began, Christ completed.

After Jesus' sacrifice there would be no more need to shed blood. "Christ entered the Most Holy Place only once—

Innocent blood was offered, once and for all time.

and for all time. He did not take with him the blood of goats and calves. His sacrifice was his own blood. He entered the Most Holy Place and set us free from sin forever" (Hebrews 9:12 ICB).

The Son of God became the Lamb of God, the cross became the altar, and we were "made holy through the sacrifice of his body. Christ made this sacrifice only once, and for all time" (Hebrews 10:10 ICB).

What needed to be paid was paid. What had to be done was done. Innocent blood was required. Innocent blood was offered, once and for all time. Bury those five words deep in your heart. *Once and for all time.* Because what they tell you is this: You do not earn salvation. Jesus has already earned it for you. Salvation is yours. The gift has been given for you to accept.

Lauren stood at the foot of the long aisle. Waiting. She smoothed the skirt of the pink gown one last time, then shook back her long dark hair threaded with dozens of narrow pink ribbons. Waiting in the silence. Then she jumped, as a jubilant thunder of sound filled the crowded church and the wedding march began.

Okay, here goes. With a last loving glance over her shoulder, she started down the aisle, scattering rose petals—pink, of course!—as she went. Behind her came the bride. Ahead of her waited the groom.

And *such* a bride and groom!

Practically skipping through the rose petals—trailing yards and yards of white satin and lace—the silver-haired bride came joyfully down the aisle. With every step her beaming smile grew a little bigger. There at the altar, waiting for his "darling Amy"—bald head gleaming under the sanctuary lights, and looking only *slightly* uncomfortable in his rented tuxedo—stood the groom.

Lauren's grandparents—her lovely, quirky, wonderful grandparents—were getting married. Again. On their fiftieth wedding anniversary.

Which Lauren wasn't quite sure she understood. I mean, they were already married, right? Had been for fifty years. So what was the point of—?

But never mind. It was what they wanted. And that was fine with Lauren. And it did seem to make perfect sense to *them*. "Well, you know, dear, we always like to do something a little special to celebrate."

Well, when it came to special, this certainly took the cake. The wedding cake. Still, Lauren couldn't help but wonder why they were doing what was already . . . *done.*

>>>>>>>>>>>>>>>>>>>>>>>>>>>>

God's work *for* us has already been done. Just as the victory of your winning team is credited to you, too, so the victory of Jesus' blood is credited to us. But that's only *part* of the story.

Remember what else happens when you play on a team? You improve. You *change.* And just as your skills improve through the influence of your team, your life can improve the longer and closer you walk with Jesus. The work *for* us is complete. But the work *in* us? Ah, that goes on . . . and on . . . and on.

We see his work for us in the blood that was shed at the cross. And in the water that flowed from his side, we see . . .

God's work in us.

Remember the words of Jesus to the Samaritan woman? "The water I give will become a spring of water gushing up inside that person, giving eternal life" (John 4:14). Jesus offers not a singular drink of water, but an ever-flowing well! And the well isn't a hole in your backyard, but the Holy Spirit of God in your heart.

> "If a person believes in me, rivers of living water will flow out
> from his heart. This is what the Scripture says." Jesus was
> talking about the Holy Spirit. The Spirit had not yet been

given because Jesus had not yet been raised to glory. But later, those who believed in Jesus would receive the Spirit. (John 7:38–39 ICB)

Water, in this verse, is a picture of the Spirit of Jesus working *in* us. Jesus cleanses us, refreshes us, and energizes us. He's not working to save us, mind you; that work is done. He's working to change us. Here's how Paul described the process.

> Do the good things that *result from being saved*, obeying God with deep reverence, *shrinking back from all that might displease him. For God is at work within you,* helping you want to obey him, and then helping you do what he wants.
>
> (Philippians 2:12–13 TLB, italics mine)

As a result of "being saved" (the work of the blood), what do we do? We obey God "with deep reverence" and shrink back "from all that might displease him." In other words, we love our neighbor and refrain from gossip. We refuse to cheat and do our best to love people who are tough to love. Do we do this in order to be saved? No. These are "the good things that result from being saved."

Something similar occurs in marriage. Are a bride and groom ever more married than they are the first day? The vows are made and the certificate signed—could they be any more married than that?

Maybe they could. Imagine them—like Lauren's grandparents—fifty years later. Four kids later. A trio of job transfers and a cluster of valleys and victories later. After half a century of marriage, they finish each other's sentences and order each other's food. They even start looking alike after a while. (A thought that troubles *my* wife deeply.) Wouldn't they have to be more married on their fiftieth anniversary than on their wedding day?

Yet, on the other hand, how could they be? The marriage certificate hasn't matured. Ah, but the relationship has, and there is a difference. Technically, they are no more united than they were when they left the altar. But relationally, they are completely different.

Marriage is both a done deal and a daily development, something you did and something you do.

The same is true of our walk with God.

Lauren swallowed a bite of strawberry wedding cake and looked around the enormous tent with delighted eyes. Wedding guests chattered and danced. Jugglers juggled. Tumblers tumbled. Clowns . . . clowned. And right in the middle of it all—having the best time of all—were the bride and groom.

Lauren grinned. *Leave it to Gram and Gramps to hire a circus for their wedding reception. Their* second *wedding—*which reminded her . . .

Lauren slipped through the crowd—carefully dodging the fire-eater—and slid an arm around her grandfather's waist.

"Gramps," she said, with a quick peck on the cheek, "there's just one thing I don't understand . . ."

"Only one?" he teased. "That's pretty impressive for thirteen."

Lauren giggled. "No, really. You and Grandma Amy have been married for fifty years. So why this? Are you *more* married now?"

He hugged Lauren and smiled across the room at his bride. "Sweetie, your grandma and I get a little *more* married every day! That's the wonderful thing about relationships. They're always growing and changing—unfolding lovely new surprises. Like you."

"Me?"

"Well, of course *you*. You're very much a part of our relationship *now*. But when it all started fifty years ago you were only a beautiful thought in God's mind." He tweaked one of the pink ribbons in her hair. "Kinda makes you think, doesn't it?"

Can you be more saved than you were on the first day of your salvation? No. But can a person grow in salvation? Absolutely. It, like marriage, is a done deal and a daily development.

The blood is God's sacrifice for us.

The water is God's Spirit in us.

And we need both. John is very concerned that we know this. It's not enough to know *what* came forth; we must know *how* they came forth: "At once blood and water came out" (John 19:34). John doesn't emphasize one over the other. But, oh, how *we* do.

Some accept the blood but forget the water. They want to be saved but don't want to be changed.

Others accept the water but forget the blood. They are busy for Christ but never at peace in Christ.

What about you? Do you tend to lean one way or the other?

Do you feel so saved that you never serve? Are you so happy with the score of your team that you never want to leave the playing field? If so, let me ask a question. Why does God have you on the field in the first place? Why didn't he beam you up the moment he saved you? The fact is, you and I are here for a reason, and that reason is to glorify God in our service.

Or is your tendency the opposite? Maybe you always serve for fear of not being saved. Perhaps you don't trust your team. You're worried that your mistakes *will* count against you—might even get you cut from the team. If that's you, know this: The blood of Jesus is enough to save you.

Engrave in your heart the announcement of John the Baptist: Jesus is "the Lamb of God, who takes away the sin of the world" (John 1:29). You are *already* saved. That will never change. But you can. And should.

You can open yourself to God's Spirit working *in* you. Stretch. Grow. Change. And become *everything* that he intends you to be.

The fact is, you and I are here for a reason...

12

Tender Love. Tough Love. *True* Love.

"I Will Love You Forever"
(God's Promise in the Cross)

For God loved the world so much that he gave his only Son. God gave his Son so that whoever believes in him may not be lost, but have eternal life.

JOHN 3:16 ICB

True love is God's love for us, not our love for God. God sent his Son to be the way to take away our sins.

1 JOHN 4:10 ICB

Christ had no sin. But God made him become sin. God did this for us so that in Christ we could become right with God.

2 CORINTHIANS 5:21 ICB

Zeke smiled as he looked at the faded snapshot pinned to his bulletin board. *What were we, two . . . three . . . years old?* Two little kids, faces smeared with chocolate from somebody's birthday cake. Tony and "Eeek-yo" (which was as close as Tony could come to "Ezekiel" when they'd first met in the sandbox at day care).

They'd soon compromised on "Zeke." And it stuck. Of course, Tony had called him lots of other things, too, over the years between play school and middle school. "Hurry-up!-Zeke," "Look-at-this-Zeke," "Zeke-Old-Buddy," "Zeke-the-Magnificent," even (for a mercifully short time) "El Zeako." But whatever else he'd called him, Tony had *always* called him . . . friend.

But maybe not for much longer. Zeke had a problem.

How *do* you tell your best friend that he's acting like a . . . well, like a . . . jerk?! Or *do* you tell him at all?

Wouldn't it be kinder just not to notice? To give him space to work things out? To stick with him through thick and thin— though Tony *was* stretching "thin" way past the breaking point—just like always?

On the other hand, was it fair *not* to tell him? To let him just keep on piling mistake on top of mistake?

We all face moments in life when we must choose between doing the kind thing or the *right* thing. Do we tell a friend the truth, and risk hurt feelings? Or do we just look the other way, and let the mistakes fall where they may?

On a much grander scale, God faces with humankind what Zeke faced with the crisis in his friend Tony's life. How can he be both just and kind? How can he give both truth and mercy? How can he redeem the sinner without endorsing the sin?

Can a holy God overlook our mistakes?

Can a kind God punish our mistakes?

From our point of view there are only two equally unappealing solutions. But from where God sits, there is a third. It's called "the Cross of Christ." And it's the place where God brought justice *and* mercy into perfect harmony.

Zeke was no closer to an answer to help Tony now than he was a month ago. And he was getting pretty tired of trying to figure it out! In fact, he was really tempted to just do what it seemed like Tony wanted *everyone* to do—just leave him alone! *And he's doing a great job of making that happen!* Today was just about the last straw—

Hey, cut the guy a little slack. He's your best friend, remember? That he was, and it hurt Zeke to see Tony hurting so much. His parents' divorce had hit him really hard. So hard, in fact, that Tony had become almost an entirely different person. The honor roll student had stopped caring about his grades—didn't even bother with homework anymore. The star of the soccer team cut more practices than he showed up for. And when he *did* show up, he seemed determined to be the nastiest, meanest player on the field. And the good-natured kid with the big smile? Well, *he'd* turned into someone who treated his friends like . . . dirt.

Even his *best* friend— which hurt more than Zeke liked to admit. And he'd tried everything he could think of to help Tony get through this hard time. But none of it seemed to make the least difference. When he tried talking, Tony wasn't in the mood to listen. When he offered to listen, Tony wasn't in the mood to talk. And he graciously ignored a lot of pretty bad attitude. He *wanted* to "be there" for his friend, but Tony wasn't buying any of it. To be fair, Zeke had to admit he had no idea how he would act if his family were splitting right down the middle. And if he were caught in that middle, like Tony.

Tony's parents tried to make it a "friendly" divorce. But each felt it was really the other person's fault. And that showed. And then there was the matter of whom Tony would live with. They both wanted him. But Tony—who blamed them *both*—didn't want to live with either one. Though he *did* have to choose.

...he'd turned into someone who treated his friends like... dirt.

So choose he would. And had. But it was what he chose—
and why—that really had Zeke steamed! And confused. Caught
between what was kind, and what was right. Trying to go in
two directions at once. At cross-purposes, you might say.

The cross. Can you turn in any direction without seeing one? Perched
atop a chapel. Carved into a graveyard headstone. Engraved in a ring
or hanging on a chain. The cross is the universal symbol of Christianity.
An odd choice, don't you think? Strange that a tool of torture could
come to embody a movement of hope. The symbols of other faiths
are more upbeat: the six-pointed star of David, the crescent moon of
Islam, a lotus blossom of Buddhism. Yet a cross for Christianity? An
instrument of execution?

Would you wear a tiny electric chair around your neck? Suspend
a gold-plated hangman's noose on the wall? Would you print a picture
of a firing squad on a business card? Yet we do all those things with
the cross. Many even make the sign of the cross as they pray. Would
we make the sign of, say, a guillotine? Instead of the triangular touch
on the forehead and shoulders, how about a karate chop on the
palm? Doesn't quite have the same feel, does it?

Why is the cross the symbol of our faith? To find the answer
look no farther than the cross itself. Its design couldn't be simpler.
One beam horizontal—the other vertical. One reaches out—like
God's love. The other reaches up—as does God's holiness. One
shows us the width of his love; the other the height of his holiness.

The cross is the intersection. The cross is where God forgave his children without lowering his standards.

The standards Tony used in making his choice about where to live couldn't have been any lower. Because they were intended to cause the most hurt to everyone involved. Including Tony—not that *that* seemed to matter a bit.

"Yup, made up my mind," he'd told Zeke that afternoon. "Gonna live with my dad."

Zeke was amazed. He knew Tony adored his mother. "I thought you and your dad didn't get along all that well—except when you win a soccer game."

"We don't," Tony confirmed with a gleam in his eye.

Zeke tried again. "And don't you always complain that he never seems to have time for you?"

"He doesn't." Tony grinned. "That's the beauty of it, my man."

"But what about your mom?" Zeke knew how close they were.

Tony shrugged. "What about her? She'll get over it. Besides, she's always on my case about something. 'Homework done?' 'What about your chores?' 'Really, Tony, you need your sleep. Lights out at ten, mister!' Like she really *cares* . . ." Tony's voice shook just a little on that last word. And were those tears in his eyes?

Tony stood up and walked over to look out the window.

"Now my dad, on the other hand, won't notice *what* I do. Think about it, Zeke: freedom!"

Zeke wasn't at all convinced. And he wasn't so sure Tony was, either. "But that'll mean you'll be living clear across town. Going to a different school. What about all your friends . . . ?" *What about me?* was what he meant.

Tony just stared out the window for a long time, then he answered: "Hey, things change. I've sure learned *that!*"

Zeke didn't know what to say. But he tried. "Well . . . I guess that'll make your dad happy."

Tony laughed. "Oh, I wouldn't count on that. You know that 'my-son-the-soccer-star' thing he enjoys so much?"

Zeke nodded. Soccer was the one thing that really brought Tony and his dad together.

"Giving it up. Like I said, things change."

Zeke was stunned. His mom. His school. His friends. And now, soccer. Tony was trashing it all! *Well, that'll show us! Show us all. If Tony feels bad, everyone else is going to feel even worse! What kind of standards are those?!* And that was when Zeke started to get pretty mad himself.

G od forgave his children without lowering his standards . . . How could he do this? In a sentence: God put our sin on his Son and punished it there.

"God put on him the wrong who never did anything wrong, so we could be put right with God" (2 Corinthians 5:21 MSG).

Or as said elsewhere: "Christ never sinned! But God treated him as a sinner, so that Christ could make us acceptable to God" (CEV).

Picture the moment. God on his throne. You on the earth. And between you and God—suspended between you and heaven—is Christ on his cross. Your sins have been placed on Jesus. God, who punishes sin, releases his rightful wrath on your mistakes. Jesus receives the blow. Since Christ is between you and God, you don't. The sin is punished, but you are safe—safe in the shadow of the cross.

This is what God did, but why, why would he do it? Moral duty? Heavenly obligation? Fatherly requirement? No. God is required to do nothing.

Besides, consider what he did. He gave his Son. His only Son. Would you do that? If you had a child, would you offer his or her life for someone else? I wouldn't. There are those for whom I would give my life. But ask me to make a list of those for whom I would kill my daughter? The sheet will be blank. I don't need a pencil. The list has no names.

But God's list contains the name of every person who ever lived. For this is the scope of his love. And this is the reason for the cross. He loves the world.

God forgave his children without lowering his standards.

"For God so loved the world that he gave his only Son" (John 3:16 NLT).

As boldly as the upright beam proclaims God's holiness, the cross-beam declares his love. And, oh, how wide his love reaches.

Aren't you glad the verse does not read:

"For God so loved the rich . . ."?

Or, "For God so loved the famous . . ."?

Or, "For God so loved the thin . . ."?

It doesn't. Nor does it state, "For God so loved the Europeans or Africans . . ."; ". . . the sober or successful . . ."; ". . . the young or the old . . ."

No, when we read John 3:16, we simply (and happily) read, "For God so loved the world."

How wide is God's love? Wide enough for the whole world. Are you included in the world? Then you are included in God's love.

It's nice to be included. You aren't always. Colleges exclude you if you aren't smart enough. Other people may exclude you if you aren't "cool" enough, and, sadly, some churches exclude you if you aren't good enough.

But though *they* may exclude you, Christ includes you. When asked to describe the width of his love, he stretched one hand to the right and the other to the left and had them nailed in that position so you would know he died loving you.

But isn't there a limit? Surely there has to be an end to this love. You'd think so, wouldn't you? But David the adulterer never found it.

Paul the murderer never found it. Peter the liar never found it. When it came to life, they hit bottom. But when it came to God's love, they never did.

They, like you, found their names on God's list of love. Because he wrote it there—at the cross.

Zeke didn't stay mad long, of course. He knew Tony was really hurting. But making important choices based on how much he could make everyone else hurt, too, was just plain . . . dumb!

Worse than dumb, actually. Because not one of the things Tony was doing would make *him* feel the least bit better. *Going from bad to worse is not the answer!*

Yes, Tony was hurting. Yes, Tony was angry. And, yes, he probably had a right to feel both those things. But piling hurt on hurt, instead of looking for a way to heal? *No way! Only a . . . jerk would do that. And only another jerk would let his best friend get away with it!*

Which is why a very surprised Tony was brought over to Zeke's house after school, set firmly down, and nailed by a pair of determined eyes.

"Okay, friend," said Zeke, "you're big on change these days, so let's talk about change. Starting with *your* attitude!"

That got Tony's attention. Good . . . 'bout time something did!

Zeke held up his hand as an indignant Tony opened his mouth. "Look, buddy, I know things are rough right now. But you've got a lot of friends—including me at the head of the line—who want to help you through it. *If* you'll let us!

"We're there for you . . . unless you drive us away. And you're doing a really good job of that!"

Tony stared at his friend for a long time, then the anger on his face changed to . . . embarrassment. "Yeah," he said, "I am, aren't I? But I can't seem to help myself."

"Well, I know someone who can," said Zeke, with a friendly punch on the arm. "They've got a counseling program at school for kids going through this very thing. And you're signed up to meet with Mrs. Adams tomorrow at four! And I'll go with you every week . . . for as long as it takes. Deal?" he asked with a hopeful smile.

Zeke held his breath as Tony thought it over for what seemed like forever. Then . . .

"Deal, El Zeako," came the reply.

And that was when the healing began. For Tony, *and* his friends.

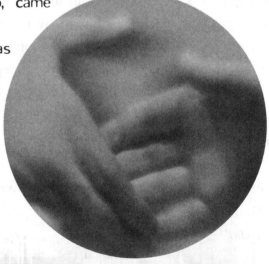

No Place to Go But . . . Up!

"I Can Turn Your Tragedy into Triumph"
(God's Promise in the Burial Clothing)

Yet, O LORD, you are our Father; we are the clay, and you are our potter; we are all the work of your hand.

ISAIAH 64:8 NRSV

I can do all things through Christ because he gives me strength.

PHILIPPIANS 4:13 ICB

Yes, you will suffer for a short time. But after that, God will make everything right. He will make you strong. He will support you and keep you from falling. He is the God who gives all grace. He called you to share in his glory in Christ. That glory will continue forever.

I PETER 5:10 ICB

What do you say we have a chat about graveclothes? Sound like fun? Sound like a cheery topic? Hardly. Make a list of depressing subjects, and burial garments is somewhere between final exams and being fitted for braces.

No one likes graveclothes. No one discusses graveclothes. Have you ever spiced up chats with your friends with the question "What are you planning to wear in your casket?"

Most folks don't discuss graveclothes.

The apostle John, however, was an exception. Ask him, and he'll tell you how he came to see burial garments as a symbol of triumph. He didn't always see them that way. A painful reminder of the death of his best friend, Jesus, they used to seem like a symbol of tragedy. But on the first Easter Sunday, God took clothing of death and made it a symbol of life.

Could he do the same for you?

Sooner or later, we all face tragedy. What's more, we all at some time or another receive the symbols of tragedy. Yours might be an ID bracelet from the hospital, a scar, or a newspaper clipping about a friend's death. We don't like these symbols, nor do we want these symbols. Like wrecked cars in a junkyard, they clutter up our hearts with memories of bad days.

Could God use such things for something good? How far can we go with verses like this one: "In everything God works for the good of those who love him" (Romans 8:28)? Does "everything" include tests and tempers and troubles? John would answer yes. John would tell you that *God can turn any tragedy into a triumph, if only you will wait and watch.*

Eric stood at the finish line, waiting—along with everyone else—as the last of the young racers arranged themselves at the starting line. It took awhile. But nobody in the cheering crowd minded a bit.

Eric grinned as he watched his little brother, JayJay, pick a spot . . . change his mind . . . find one he liked better. There! Everyone was ready—no, wait! One little girl couldn't seem to find a place—until JayJay moved over to make room for her. Which, of course, meant everyone else had to move, too . . . But no one in the waiting crowd minded, Eric least of all. *Take your time, JayJay, we'll wait. You're worth waiting for.*

It wasn't the first time Eric had waited for his little brother. The noise of the crowd seemed to fade away as he remembered . . .

Eric hadn't been nearly so patient then, eight years ago. But then, he was only a little kid himself. And to that six-year-old Eric, it seemed that he had been waiting *forever* for the new baby brother to be born.

"Do you think he's here *yet*, Grandma?" he asked for the umpteenth time.

"Be patient, sweetheart," said his grandmother—who hadn't been able to sit still herself for the last three hours. "All in God's good time. Remember, Eric, we can't be sure it is a boy—"

"Oh, yes," breathed Eric. "It's a boy! What would I do with a baby *sister*?! But I wish he'd *hurry!*"

His grandmother laughed and hugged him. "To tell the truth, so do I! But your daddy promised to call us from the hospital as soon as—"

Ring!

She snatched up the phone. "Hello. Peter? Oh, my, are we glad to hear from you! How is Ann? That's lovely. And the baby? . . . Tell us about the baby . . ."

Eric was bouncing up and down with excitement. His little brother was born! But . . . but why did his grandma look so sad. Why were there tears in her eyes?

"Oh, Peter . . . ," she said into the telephone. "Oh, my dear Lord. . . ."

There are times in life when great joy suddenly turns into great sorrow. And when that happens, it's easy to forget something the apostle John learned firsthand: God can turn any tragedy into triumph. To prove his point, John would tell you about one Friday in particular.

> Later, a man named Joseph from Arimathea asked Pilate if he
> could take the body of Jesus. (Joseph was a secret follower
> of Jesus, because he was afraid of the Jews.) Pilate gave his
> permission. So Joseph came and took Jesus' body away.
> Nicodemus went with Joseph. Nicodemus was the man who
> earlier had come to Jesus at night. He brought about 75
> pounds of spices. This was a mixture of myrrh and aloes. These
> two men took Jesus' body and wrapped it with the spices in
> pieces of linen cloth. (This is how the Jews bury people.)
> (John 19:38–40 ICB)

Fearful during Christ's life but courageous at his death, Joseph and
Nicodemus came to serve Jesus. They came to bury him. They climbed
the hill bearing the burial clothing.

Pilate had given his permission.

Joseph of Arimathea had given a tomb.

Nicodemus had brought the spices and linens.

John tells us that Nicodemus brought
seventy-five pounds of myrrh and
aloes. The amount is worth noting,
for such a great quantity of burial
ointments was usually used only
for kings. John also comments on
the linens because to him they
were a picture of Friday's tragedy. As
long as there were no graveclothes, as
long as there was no tomb, there was hope.

Friday's tragedy would be Sunday's triumph.

But the arrival of the spices and linens signaled the departure of any hope. To this apostle, the graveclothes symbolized tragedy.

Could there have been a greater tragedy for John than a dead Jesus? Three years earlier John had turned his back on his career and cast his lot with this Nazarene carpenter. Earlier in the week John had enjoyed a ticker-tape parade as Jesus and the disciples entered Jerusalem. Oh, how quickly things had turned! The people who had called him king on Sunday called for his death the following Friday. These linens were a visible reminder that his friend and future were wrapped in cloth and sealed behind a rock.

John didn't know on that Friday what you and I now know. He didn't know that Friday's tragedy would be Sunday's triumph. John later confesses that he "did not yet understand from the Scriptures that Jesus must rise from the dead" (John 20:9).

That's why what John did on Saturday is so important.

He waited.

When Eric's mother first explained about his new baby brother, it didn't make a lot of sense to him.

"JayJay's a very . . . *special* child, Eric." Eric nodded happily. Of course he was. He was his baby brother! And Eric had so much to show him and tell him and teach him . . .

"He's not like other children, and he's *never* going to be like other children." Now, that was confusing. Looked like a perfectly good baby to him!

"Sweetheart, when God made JayJay, he made him just a little bit . . . different. Some things inside him just don't work as well for him as they do for other people. And some things that are easy for other kids to learn and do will be very hard for JayJay. But God has his reasons. God always has his reasons . . ."

Of course, most of that went right over Eric's head. When you're only six, words like "Down syndrome" don't mean very much.

But they meant a great deal to his parents' friends.

"Oh, how sad . . ."

"Ann, I'm so sorry!"

"Such a tragedy . . ."

"NO!" said Eric's mother. "Not a tragedy. A gift! God made JayJay special for a reason. And he gave him to us for a reason. Wait and see."

Is there anything harder than waiting? Especially when you don't know what you're waiting for? The apostle John would probably tell you there isn't.

We don't know anything about that Saturday after Jesus' death. We have no passage to read, no knowledge to share. All we know is this: When Sunday came, John was still present. When Mary Magdalene came looking for him, she found him.

Jesus was dead. The Master's body was lifeless. John's friend and future were buried. But John had not left. Why? Was he waiting for the resurrection? No. As far as he knew, the lips were forever silent and the hand forever still. He wasn't expecting a Sunday surprise. Then why was he there?

You'd think he would have left. Who was to say the men who crucified Christ wouldn't come after him? Why didn't John get out of town?

Perhaps the answer was very ordinary; perhaps he was taking care of Jesus' mother. Or perhaps he didn't have anywhere else to go. Could be, he didn't have any money or energy or direction . . . or all of the above.

Or maybe he lingered because he loved Jesus.

To others, Jesus was a miracle worker. To others, Jesus was a master teacher. To others, Jesus was the hope of Israel. But to John, he was all of these and more. To John, Jesus was a friend.

You don't abandon a friend—not even when that friend is dead. John stayed close to Jesus.

He had a habit of doing this. He was close to Jesus in the Upper Room. He was close to Jesus in the Garden of Gethsemane. He was at the foot of the cross at the crucifixion, and he was a quick walk from the tomb at the burial.

Did he understand Jesus? No.

Was he glad Jesus did what he did? No.

But did he leave Jesus? No.

What about you? When you're in John's

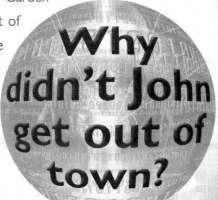

Why didn't John get out of town?

position, what do you do? When it's Saturday in your life, how do you react? When you are somewhere between yesterday's tragedy and tomorrow's triumph, what do you do? Do you leave God—or do you linger near him?

"BANG!"

The crack of the starter's pistol brought Eric back from the past in a flash. The race was on! And here they came . . . fifteen excited little kids chugging down the track as fast as they could. (Which wasn't all that fast. Not that anyone minded. As far as the cheering crowd was concerned, these Special Athletes had *wings* on their heels!) And right in the middle of the pack—arms pumping, face beaming with joy—came eight-year-old JayJay.

"Go, JayJay . . . Go, Little Bro!"

And, somehow, in all the roar of the crowd JayJay heard his big brother's voice. And his smile grew even wider. It had always been that way. From the time he was a baby, his big blue eyes would shine like stars the moment Eric walked into the room. He sat up for the first time—a lot later than babies usually do—for Eric. He took his first staggering steps—way later than most toddlers do—for Eric. And his very first word—long after everyone had given up on him ever talking—was "Ric . . . Ric."

For a long time, Eric was sure everyone was wrong about JayJay. He *was* just like other kids. But by the time his adoring little brother was five and Eric was eleven, he had to admit the truth. JayJay *was* different. But by then it didn't matter.

Yes, there were things he'd never be able to do or understand. But, oh, he knew how to try. And, oh, he knew how to laugh. And, most of all . . . oh, he knew how to *love!*

JayJay was filled to the brim—and overflowing—with love. Unquestioning . . . unconditional . . . love. The truth was, JayJay was in love with the whole world, and with everyone (especially Eric) and everything in it. Every day for JayJay was filled with joy and wonder. And it rubbed off on everyone around him. Being with JayJay just made you feel good. And when you saw the world through his shining blue eyes, you saw things—and people—in an entirely different light. Maybe the way God himself saw them.

Yes, JayJay *was* a "special needs" kid, but as far as Eric was concerned, he was a lot more special than he was needy. And he gave so much more than he ever took.

And that would have been enough. More than enough.

But JayJay was full of surprises. Who would have guessed, until last year, that the little boy who found so many things so difficult knew *exactly* how to be a hero?!

Sometimes the most amazing things happen when you least expect them. The apostle John certainly wasn't expecting anything wonderful that Saturday after the crucifixion. He wasn't waiting for anything. What was there to wait for? Jesus was dead. But John chose to linger.

To stay near Jesus. And because he lingered on Saturday, he was around on Sunday to see the miracle.

So Mary ran to Simon Peter and the other follower (the one Jesus loved). Mary said, "They have taken the Lord out of the tomb. We don't know where they have put him."

So Peter and the other follower started for the tomb. They were both running, but the other follower ran faster than Peter. So the other follower reached the tomb first. He bent down and looked in. He saw the strips of linen cloth lying there, but he did not go in. Then following him came Simon Peter. He went into the tomb and saw the strips of linen lying there. He also saw the cloth that had been around Jesus' head. The cloth was folded up and laid in a different place from the strips of linen. Then the other follower, who had reached the tomb first, also went in. He saw and believed. (John 20:2–8 ICB)

What he saw so stunned him he froze at the entrance.

Very early on Sunday morning Peter and John were given the news: "Jesus' body is missing!" Mary was frantic because she thought Jesus' enemies had taken his body away. Instantly, the two disciples hurried to the sepulcher, John outrunning Peter and arriving first. What he saw so stunned him he froze at the entrance.

What did he see? "Strips of linen cloth." He saw "the cloth that had been around Jesus' head ... folded up and laid in a different place from the strips of linen."

These burial wraps had not been ripped off and thrown down. The linens were undisturbed. The cloth for Jesus' head was neatly folded.

How could this be?

If friends had removed the body, would they not have taken the clothes with it?

If enemies had taken the body, would they not have done the same? If not, if for some reason friends or foes had unwrapped the body, would they have been so careful as to dispose of the clothing in such an orderly fashion? Of course not!

But if neither friend nor foe took the body, who did?

This was John's question, and this question led to John's discovery. "He saw and believed" (John 20:8).

Through the rags of death, John saw the power of life. Odd, don't you think, that God would use something as sad as a burial wrap to change a life?

But God is given to such practices:

- In his hand empty wine jugs at a wedding become a symbol of power.

- The coin of a widow becomes a symbol of generosity.

- A crude manger in Bethlehem is his symbol of devotion.

- And a tool of death is a symbol of his love.

Should we be surprised that he takes the wrappings of death and makes them the picture of life?

Which takes us back to the question: Could God do something similar in your life? Could he take what today is a token of tragedy and turn it into a symbol of triumph?

Could such a change happen for you? I have no doubt. You simply need to do what John did. Don't leave. Hang around.

Remember the second half of the passage, "God works for the good of *those who love him*" (Romans 8:28, italics mine). That's how John felt about Jesus. He loved him. He didn't understand him or always agree with him, but he loved him.

And because he loved him, he stayed near him. And he was there when the world changed forever.

"C'mon, JayJay. You're doing great!" Eric cheered, as the runners neared the finish line. His little brother was trailing the rest. But you'd never know that from the big grin he was wearing . . . or the way he was trying. First or last, it didn't make a bit of difference to JayJay. He *always* threw his heart over the finish line. Just as he had last year . . .

It had been a really *dumb* accident. Eric was the first to admit that. Who'd have thought that slicing a loaf of crusty bread to make sandwiches could be so . . . dangerous? Of course, holding the bread under one arm and pulling the big, sharp(!) knife *toward* himself wasn't very bright. Especially when it slipped . . .

There was blood everywhere. It poured, it gushed, it *sprayed!* Eric had sliced into the artery in his wrist. He was too dizzy to move. And he was home alone with JayJay!

Eric didn't know what might have happened if his little brother hadn't wandered into the kitchen just then. JayJay's eyes were enormous as he looked at his brother slumped on the floor—blood spurting out of his wrist, painting the cabinet doors bright red. "Oh!" he said. "Oh!" Then, "Don't worry, Eric, I know what to do. I know . . ." And he ran to the phone . . . and dialed 911. "Come fast. Come fast. Eric's bleeding all over . . . !"

The jagged scar on Eric's wrist gleamed white in his tanned skin, as he opened his arms wide at the finish line. Heading straight for him—grinning as if he'd come in first instead of dead last—was JayJay.

"Did you see me, Eric? Did you see me?"

Eric hugged him tight. "I saw you, Little Bro. I saw you."

"Was I good? Was I . . . ?"

Big hand slapped against small hand in a jubilant high-five. "You were better than good, JayJay. You were wonderful!" *And so he was*, thought Eric. Full of wonder. And wonders.

The Bible says that "in everything God works for the good of those who love him." Before we close this chapter, do this simple exercise. Take away the word *everything*, and replace it with the symbol of your tragedy. For the apostle John, the verse would read: "In *burial clothing* God works for the good of those who love him." For Eric and his family it would read: "In *a special needs child* God works for the good of those who love him."

How would Romans 8:28 read in your life?

- *In failing grades* God works for the good.

- *In the divorce of parents* God works for the good.

- *In a broken friendship* God works for the good.

If God can change John's life through a tragedy, could it be he will use a tragedy to change yours?

As hard as it may be to believe when things seem darkest, you could be only a Saturday away from a resurrection. You could be only hours from that precious prayer of a changed heart: "God, did you do this for me?"

Against All Odds!

"I Have Won the Victory"
(God's Promise in the Empty Tomb)

With the cross, [God] won the victory.

COLOSSIANS 2:15

But now in a single victorious
stroke of Life, all three—sin, guilt, death—are gone,
the gift of our Master, Jesus Christ. Thank God!

1 CORINTHIANS 15:57 MSG

But thanks be to God,
who always leads us in
victory through Christ.

2 CORINTHIANS 2:14

Ever notice how everything in life seems to be measured . . . counted . . . studied . . . graded . . . by somebody, somewhere? From that B minus on your language arts paper to the exit polls of a presidential election, somebody . . . somewhere, is keeping score.

Numbers. Statistics. Surveys. Opinion polls. Everybody uses them. A lot of people rely on them. And they can supply valuable information. Tell you a lot. But there's one thing that numbers and opinions can't always accurately measure: truth.

You have to look a lot deeper than surface appearances for that. Because truth doesn't care what anyone—or everyone—thinks or says or does. It simply is. Which, from time to time, leaves a lot of people with a lot of egg on their faces.

Let's face it, "Most Likely to Succeed" is not the prediction anyone—except God—would have made for the baby born in Bethlehem some two thousand years ago!

HIS BIRTH

The words of King Herod when told of the birth of Jesus: *"Kill him. There is room for only one king in this corner of the world."*

The number of religious leaders who believed a messiah had been born in Bethlehem: *Zero.*

The type of people who did believe: *Some stargazers, night-shift shepherds, and a couple of newlyweds.*

The reward given to Joseph and Mary for bringing God into the world: *Two years in exile, learning Egyptian.*

This was the beginning of the Christian movement. *(And these were the calm years.)*

If you asked anyone who knew the bare facts of Jez Marshall's childhood what *her* chances were, the answer would probably be a sad shake of the head.

From the time she was three, Jez and her mother were part of the "invisible" population—fallen through the cracks—of a big, indifferent city. When her mother was well enough to work—and could *find* a job—they lived in a series of bleak public housing apartments. In between, there were a lot of nights spent in their old rattletrap of a car—and more than a few in homeless shelters.

Then, when Jez was eight, the worst happened. Her gentle, fragile mother—who had always done the best she could for Jez—collapsed in the diner where she'd just started a new job. She never came home from the hospital. And a bewildered, grieving Jez was sent to live in the first of a series of foster homes.

Those are the facts. But behind the *facts,* as it always does, lies another story.

True, when it came to material things, Jez's mother had very little to offer her precious daughter. But she did have three gifts to give. And she gave them lavishly. Love. Faith. Hope.

"You are the best—the very best—thing that ever happened to me, sweetie!" her mom would say. Jez knew beyond a shadow of a doubt that she was well and truly loved—and was *worthy* of love. (And if other people couldn't see that, as far as Jez was concerned, that was *their* problem!)

"Always keep your chin up, punkin'. It's not what you have that matters, it's who you are. And *you* are special. Believe in yourself!" So Jez looked the world straight in the eye and made absolutely no apologies for anything. (And if that made some people nervous, well, that was their problem.)

"But you *do* have a Father, lovey," her mother answered when Jez asked why she didn't have a daddy. "You have a Father in heaven who loves you beyond imagining and will always take care of you." (Jez liked that idea a lot. Though she did—wrongly!—figure God must be pretty busy—and probably counted on her to pretty much take care of things for herself.)

Jez held on to... Her mother's love. Faith in herself. Trust in God.

In the years that followed—in foster home after foster home, school after school—these were the things Jez held on to. Her mother's love. Faith in herself. Trust in God—who had given her a very special gift of his own . . .

No, the Jez Marshall—with the outrageous black wardrobe and independent attitude—who turned heads in the Jefferson Middle School cafeteria one bright October day was not your *ordinary* thirteen-year-old. Jenny Archer and her friends may have wondered about her . . . but Jez knew *exactly* who she was. And what other people thought was *their* problem.

HIS MINISTRY

The word on the streets of Jesus' hometown when he claimed to be sent from God: *Weird family. Have you seen his cousin?*

The reaction of the hometown folks: *Stone him.*

The opinion of his brothers: *Lock him up.*

The number of disciples Jesus recruited: *Seventy.*

The number of disciples who defended him to the authorities: *Zero.*

The assessment of Jesus' followers as found in the Jerusalem editorial page: *A group of unemployed ne'er-do-wells recruited off the shipping docks and from the "wrong" side of town.*

The number of lepers and blind and lame people Jesus healed: *Too many to count.*

The number of healed lepers and blind and lame people who defended Jesus on the day of his death: *Zero.*

"Prideful." "Difficult." "Prickly." "Impossible!" All these words had been used, at one time or another, to describe young Jez. And not entirely unfairly. The truth was, brilliant as she was in some areas, Jez had absolutely no talent at all for making friends, or "fitting in" at her various foster homes.

"My goodness, Jez," sighed Emily Harris, the social worker who had taken Jez under her wing, "you're as independent as . . . as a cat!"

Actually, Jez rather liked that idea. She admired cats a great deal. Sleek, elegant creatures who took on the world with a cool, doesn't-matter-to-me attitude. Independent spirits who went their own way, asked for—and expected—nothing from anyone. (That way you were never disappointed.)

"Well, never mind," said Ms. Harris with a smile and a hug, "the Andersons have room. And they're lovely people. If you'd just give them a chance . . ." She looked at Jez doubtfully.

"I will, I promise," said Jez, returning the hug. And she *would* try. Just to please this *one* friend she did have. Emily Harris was the one person who had—with persistence and love—seen past the cool, reserved outside to the eager, hopeful Jez inside. She was also the one who had discovered—and encouraged—Jez's amazing talent for math.

"This is an incredible gift, Jez!" she said with awe when she discovered that her young charge was working—and understanding—math problems years ahead of her age level. "A talent like this can take you as far as you want it to!"

Jez didn't see what all the fuss was about. She had always

been fascinated with numbers. She loved their polished logic and the precise—unemotional—way they worked. You didn't have to smile at, or charm, numbers. They simply were. And the things they could do . . . ! One of which, she'd decided when she was twelve, would be to take a girl from the mean streets of Chicago to . . . the stars!

...what were the chances of something that unlikely happening...?

Jez had it all planned. She'd stick out the foster home thing. Work hard in school. Figure out *some* way to get to college. Then . . . the space program!

It was all worked out. Down to the last detail. Except for that unexpected little "detour" that God—and Emily Harris—had arranged. After all, what were the chances of something that unlikely happening . . . ?!

His Execution

The popular opinion regarding Jesus before he cleansed the Temple: *See if he'll run for office.*

The popular opinion regarding Jesus after he cleansed the Temple: *Let's see how fast he can run.*

The decision of the Jewish council: *Three spikes and a spear.*

The talk on the streets of Jerusalem after Jesus died: *He should've stayed in the furniture business.*

The number of times Jesus prophesied that he would come back to life three days after his death: *Three.*

The number of apostles who heard the prophecy: *All of them.*

The number of apostles who waited at the tomb to see if he would do what he said: *Zero.*

The number of his followers who believed in the resurrection before it occurred: *You do the math.*

The odds a street-corner bookie would've given the day after the crucifixion on the possibility that Jesus' name would be known in the year 2000: *"I'll give you better odds that he'll rise from the dead."*

It practically qualified as a bona fide . . . miracle. After years of searching—Emily Harris was a *very* determined social worker—she had finally found an aunt for Jez. An aunt, moreover, who was delighted to welcome the daughter of her long-lost sister into her home.

"An aunt?! I didn't know I had *any* relatives . . ." Jez was floored by the news. Her mother had never said anything about her family. Or why she left home. Except that one time . . . "Oh, I guess I'm just the black sheep in the family, sweetie." And that was good enough for Jez. If her mom was a black sheep, she'd be one, too. And *that* was when she began her love affair with clothes of basic black!

To tell the truth, Jez wasn't at all sure she was nearly as delighted as her Aunt Margaret and Emily Harris were about her new "home" in a lovely small town. She was doing just fine in Chicago! But one look into her Aunt Margaret's loving gray eyes—eyes just like her mother's—and one enormous, laughing hug, and Jez was a goner.

Of course, she and her aunt were still getting to know each other. But things at home looked good. Very good. Much better, in fact, than they did at her new school—where she'd made her usual take-me-as-I-am entrance.

Because there was still that problem of making friends. Yes, she'd like to have friends. Who wouldn't? No, she had no idea how to go about making any. And there *were* kids—like that girl in math class—who seemed pretty interesting. Jenny Archer was her name. And, as everyone else was, Jez felt drawn to her warm smile and laughing eyes. She could tell that Jenny was having trouble with today's math lesson—and not liking it one bit. So what did Jez do? Did she give her an encouraging smile? Did she offer to help? She did not!

No, I had to . . . okay, show off! Make her feel really dumb. Let her know who was the smart one here. Like a cat . . . establishing territory!

Of course, those particular chickens came right home to roost a couple of hours later at lunch. Jez stood there in the cafeteria—where everyone but her seemed to have a place— looking across the room at Jenny and her friends. (It wasn't hard to spot that burning bush of red hair.) For one moment, when Jenny's eyes met hers, she'd actually hoped that Jenny might invite her over to her table. Ha! The snub, when it came, hurt. But it wasn't really a surprise. So she just lifted her chin a little higher in the air and turned away. *Okay. Cheat yourself, Miss Popularity! What goes around comes around.*

And, amazingly, it "came around" that same afternoon. At swim team practice. There in the very next lane was Jenny Archer—one of the team stars, of course—swimming for all she was worth.

Oh no you don't! thought Jez, and put on a burst of speed she had no idea she possessed. And finished first. *So there!*

HIS MOVEMENT

The official response of the Jewish leaders to the rumors of the resurrection: *Of course they say he's alive. They have to. What else can they say?*

"If their plan comes from human authority, it will fail."

The actual response of the Jewish leaders to the resurrection of Jesus: *"A great number of the Jewish priests believed and obeyed"* (Acts 6:7).

The decision of the Jewish leaders about the church: *"If their plan comes from human authority, it will fail. But if it is from God, you will not be able to stop them"* (Acts 5:38–39).

The response of the church: *"The number of followers was growing"* (Acts 6:1).

The official response of the Jewish leaders to the conversion of Saul: *Good riddance to the former Pharisee. Won't be months before he's in jail, and then what will he do? Write letters?*

What Saul, turned Paul, understood that his former colleagues didn't: *"God gave [Jesus] as a way to forgive sin"* (Romans 3:25).

Jez pulled herself up onto the pool deck and stood watching Jenny clinging to the edge. Strangely enough, winning the race didn't feel nearly as good as she thought it would. In fact, it felt as if she had maybe lost something else. An opportunity . . .

Then Jenny did something absolutely amazing. She looked up at Jez . . . and laughed.

"Good grief, Jez," she said, when she'd caught her breath, "*please* tell me you're not a math whiz *and* champion swimmer, too!"

Oh, my. Oh, . . . MY! Was this a second chance? But could she risk it? Could she—Jez-who-walks-alone—actually make a friend? On the other hand, stranger things had been happening lately. Had God arranged this, too?

Jez looked into Jenny's laughing green eyes. And decided. She grinned back. "Naah, this was just luck. Now that math thing, though . . ." Then she leaned down and reached out a hand . . . a hand of friendship. And Jenny took it.

Who would have dreamed . . . ?!

THE MOVEMENT CONTINUES

The belief of French philosopher Voltaire: *The Bible and Christianity would pass within a hundred years. He died in 1778. The movement continues.*

The pronouncement of Friedrich Nietzsche in 1882: *"God is dead." The dawn of science, he believed, would be the doom of faith. Science has dawned; the movement continues.*

The way a Communist dictionary defined the Bible: *"It is a collection of fantastic legends without any scientific support." Communism is diminishing; the movement continues.*

The discovery made by every person who has tried to bury the faith: *The same as the one made by those who tried to bury its Founder: He won't stay in the tomb.*

The facts: *The movement has never been stronger. More than one billion Catholics and nearly as many Protestants.*

The question: *How do we explain it? Jesus was a backwater peasant. He never wrote a book, never held an office. He never journeyed more than two hundred miles from his hometown. Friends left him. One betrayed him.*

Those he helped forgot him. Prior to his death they abandoned him. But after his death they couldn't resist him. What made the difference?

The answer: *His death and resurrection. For when he died, so did your sin. And when he rose, so did your hope. For when he rose, your grave was changed from a final residence to temporary housing.*

The reason he did it: *The face in your mirror.*

The verdict after two millennia: *Herod was right: There is room for only one King.*

Check Your "Baggage" Here!

(What Will You Leave at the Cross?)

Trust the Lord with all your heart.
Don't depend on your own understanding.
Remember the Lord in everything you do.
And he will give you success.

PROVERBS 3:5–6 ICB

Give all your worries to him,
because he cares for you.

I PETER 5:7 ICB

The hill is quiet now. Not still but quiet. For the first time all day there is no noise. The clamor began to hush when the darkness—that puzzling midday darkness—fell. Like water douses a fire, the shadows doused the ridicule. No more taunts. No more jokes. No more jesting. And, in time, no more mockers. One by one the onlookers turned and began the descent.

That is, all the onlookers except you and me. We did not leave. We came to learn. And so we lingered in the semidarkness and listened. We listened to the soldiers cursing, the passersby questioning, and the women weeping. But most of all, we listened to the trio of dying men groaning. Hoarse, guttural, thirsty groans. They groaned with each rolling of the head and each move of the legs.

But as the minutes became hours, these groans faded, too. The three seemed dead. Were it not for the labored breathing, you would have thought they were.

Then he screamed. As if someone had yanked his hair, the back of his head slammed against the sign that bore his name, and he screamed. Like a dagger cuts the curtain, his scream cut the dark. Standing as straight as the nails would permit, he cried as one calling for a lost friend, *"Eloi!"*

His voice was raspy, scratchy. Reflections of the torch flame danced in his wide eyes. "My God!"

Ignoring the volcano of erupting pain, he pushed upward until his shoulders were higher than his nailed hands. "Why have you forsaken me?"

The soldiers stared. The weeping of the women ceased. One of the Pharisees sneered sarcastically, "He's calling Elijah."

No one laughed.

He'd shouted a question to the heavens, and you half expected heaven to shout one in return.

And apparently it did. For the face of Jesus softened, and an afternoon dawn broke as he spoke a final time: "It is finished. Father, into your hands I commit my spirit."

As he gave his final breath, the earth gave a sudden stir. A rock rolled, and a soldier stumbled. Then, as suddenly as the silence was broken, the silence returned.

And now all is quiet. The mocking has ceased. There is no one to mock.

The soldiers are busy with the business of cleaning up the dead. Two men have come. Dressed well and meaning well, they are given the body of Jesus.

And we are left with the relics of his death.

Three nails in a bin.

Three cross-shaped shadows.

A braided crown with scarlet tips.

Bizarre, isn't it? The thought that this blood is not man's blood but God's?

Crazy, isn't it? To think that these nails held your sins to a cross?

Absurd, don't you agree? That a scoundrel's prayer was offered and answered? Or more absurd, that another scoundrel offered no prayer at all?

Absurdities and ironies. The hill of Calvary is nothing if not both.

We would have scripted the moment differently. Ask us how a God should redeem his world, and we will show you! White horses, flashing swords. Evil flat on his back. God on his throne.

But God on a cross?

A split-lipped, puffy-eyed, blood-masked God on a cross?

Sponge thrust in his face?

Spear plunged into his side?

Dice tossed at his feet?

No, we wouldn't have written the drama of redemption this way. But, then again, we weren't asked to. These players and props were heaven-picked and God-ordained. We were not asked to design the hour.

But we have been asked to respond to it. In order for the cross of Christ to be the cross of your life, you and I need to bring something to the hill.

We have seen what Jesus brought. With scarred hands he offered forgiveness. Through torn skin he promised acceptance. He took the path to take us home. He wore our garment to give us his own. We have seen the gifts he brought.

Now we ask, what will we bring?

We aren't asked to paint the sign or carry the nails. We aren't asked to wear the spit or bear the crown. But we *are* asked to walk the path and leave something at the cross.

We don't have to, of course. Many don't.

But may I urge *you* to leave something at the cross? You can observe the cross and analyze the cross. You can read about it, even pray to it. But until you leave something there, you haven't embraced the cross.

You've seen what Christ left. Won't you leave something as well? Why don't you start with your *bad moments?*

We are asked... to leave something at the cross.

Those bad habits? Leave them at the cross. Your selfish moods and white lies? Give them to God. Your binges and bigotries? God wants them all. Every flop, every failure. He wants every single one. Why? Because he knows we can't live *with* them.

I grew up playing football in the empty field next to our house. Many a Sunday afternoon was spent imitating the gridiron heroes of the day.

Empty fields in West Texas have grass burrs. Grass burrs hurt. You can't play football without falling, and you can't fall in a West Texas field without getting stuck.

More times than I can remember I pulled myself out of a sticker patch so hopelessly covered that I had to have help. Kids don't rely on other kids to pull out grass burrs. You need someone with skill. I would limp to the house so my dad could pluck out the stickers—one by painful one.

I wasn't too bright, but I knew this: If I wanted to get back into the game, I needed to get rid of those stickers.

Every mistake in life is like a grass burr. You can't live without falling, and you can't fall without getting stuck. But guess what? We aren't always as smart as young ballplayers. We sometimes try to get back into the game without dealing with the stickers. It's as if we don't want anyone to know we fell, so we pretend we never did. Consequently, we live in pain. We can't walk well, sleep well, rest well. And, oh, are we touchy!

Does God want us to live like that? No way. Listen to his promise: "This is my commitment to my people: removal of their sins" (Romans 11:27 MSG).

God does more than forgive our mistakes; he removes them! We simply have to take them to him.

He not only wants the mistakes we've made, he wants the ones we *are* making! Are you making some? Are you disobedient or resentful? Are you angry or spiteful? Are you cheating at school or cheating at friendship? Are you worried or frightened by something you've done—or are thinking of doing?

If so, don't pretend nothing is wrong. Don't pretend you didn't fall. Don't try to get back in the game. Go first to God. The first step after a stumble must be in the direction of the cross. "If we confess our sins to God, he can always be trusted to forgive us and take our sins away" (1 John 1:9 CEV).

What can you leave at the cross? Why not start with your *bad moments?* You know, those things you find yourself doing that shock you, frighten you, or make you ashamed. . . .

For Jenny Archer it was a heaping helping of jealousy—with a little spite for dessert—that cast a dark shadow over a normally sunny personality. You remember Jenny—the cool, popular girl who was used to being very good at *everything* she did? Everything, that is, except math. Her frustration and anger at the new girl who was such a whiz at math were all it took to let loose the "envy beast."

It wasn't until Jenny took a good look at herself that she was able to put envy aside. And extend the hand of friendship to someone who badly needed a friend.

It was fear that tripped up Brian Parnell . . . Brian the Bold . . . Brian the Runner. Fear that made him treat a kid in a wheelchair in a way that made him very ashamed of himself. It wasn't until he got over the hurdle of worrying about doing or saying the wrong thing that he was able to see the *right* thing to do.

Mike O'Hara desperately wanted what every kid wants: to belong—to make friends. And he found some. Unfortunately, the price of their friendship was a little shoplifting. Which—though he was tempted, *very* tempted—turned out to be a little *too* high a price for Mike.

No one ever said being a kid is easy. (At least no one who has ever *been* a kid.) But you *can* give yourself a break. You can take your envy and spite and shame and temptations and put them someplace they can't hurt you. You can leave them at the cross.

And while you're at the cross, give God your *mad moments,* too. C'mon, you know you have them.

Do you know the story about the man who was bitten by the dog? When he learned the dog had rabies, he began making a list. The doctor told him there was no need to make a will, that rabies can be cured. "Oh, I'm not making a will," he replied. "I'm making a list of all the people I want to bite."

Couldn't we all make such a list? You've already learned, haven't you, that friends aren't always friendly? Teachers aren't always patient? Parents aren't always understanding?

You've already learned, haven't you, that a promise made is not always a promise kept? That just because someone is called your parent, it doesn't mean he or she will act like a parent?

You've already learned, haven't you, that we tend to fight back? To bite back? To keep lists and snarl lips and growl at people we don't like?

God wants your list. He inspired one servant to write, "Love does not keep a record of wrongs" (1 Corinthians 13:5 TEV). He wants us to leave the list at the cross.

Not so easy to do, of course.

"Just look what they did to me!" we defy and point to our hurts.

"Just look what I did for you," he reminds and points to the cross.

Paul said it this way: "If someone does wrong to you, forgive that person because the Lord forgave you" (Colossians 3:13).

You and I are commanded—not urged, *commanded*—to keep no list of wrongs.

Besides, do you really want to keep one? Do you really want to catalog all your mistreatments? Do you really want to growl and snap your way through life? God does not want you to, either. He wants you to give up your sins before they infect you, and your bitterness and anger before they twist and maim you. And he's given you a place to do that. At the cross.

When Kim Nakamura let the cat out of the bag about her best friend's family secret, Molly Craig was not only embarrassed, she was *furious!* No, she was beyond furious— she just didn't have a word for it. Molly's anger nearly ripped apart a friendship that had made Molly and Kim practically legends in their own time. Nearly. Until Molly was reminded of something else we learn at the cross: forgiveness.

Anger over her father's disapproval of a boyfriend drove Madeline from her home . . . her hometown . . . and into a life she didn't expect. Or like. Pride and shame kept her there. Until a father's love reached out and invited her home. A Father's love waits at the cross, too. Along with a place for *everything* that troubles or burdens us. . . .

There's something else you can leave at the cross, too. Your sorrow and pain. Sometimes things happen to us that are outside our control.

Things that hurt us deeply, though they are not our fault at all. Jesus will carry your sad moments for you, too. If you let him.

Jez Marshall's trust in God's love carried her through some very sad times after her mother's death and during her years in a series of foster homes. But it wasn't until she let go of her fear of rejection—not that Jez would admit to being afraid of *anything!*—that she was able to reach out for the friendship she craved.

When the door closed on Nicole's dream of a career as a ballet dancer, she was heartbroken. But when she looked beyond her pain and disappointment—and gave up her anger and sorrow—she saw that God was holding *another* door wide open for her!

For Eric, a little brother with a serious disability *could* have been seen as a tragedy. But it's pretty hard to stay sad when you trust in God—and live in the same house as pure, unconditional *love.*

God knows exactly what to do with the saddest, most painful moments in *your* life, too.

Or maybe you're worried . . . uncertain . . . fearful . . . about something. You don't have to be, you know. There's someone waiting at the cross to take those things from you. God wants your *anxious moments,* too.

If you were to look very carefully at the foot of the cross, you'd see all kinds of worrisome, troubling things that people no longer needed.

You might find the painful shyness that doesn't "fit" David anymore. Or the excuses Josh *could* have made, instead of finding a creative way to come up with a special gift for a special someone.

Could be you might trip over Kyle's brash certainty that he *always* knew best. (He swapped that for a dash of humility.)

And—right over there—the fear of losing a friendship that Zeke traded in for the courage to tell his friend Tony the truth about some bad choices he was making.

And, of course, there's always room for more. Perhaps a little anxious . . . troubling . . . *something* of yours?

Next time you're convinced that your world is about to come to an end, take a mental trip up the hill. Spend a few moments looking again at the pieces of the passion.

Run your thumb over the tip of the spear. Balance a spike in the palm of your hand. Read the wooden sign written in your own language. And as you do, touch the velvet dirt, moist with the blood of God.

Blood he bled for you.
The spear he took for you.
The nails he felt for you.
The sign he left for you.

He did all of this for you. Knowing this, knowing all he did for you there, don't you think he'll look out for you here?

Or as Paul wrote, "God did not keep back his own Son, but he gave him for us. If God did this, won't he freely give us everything else?" (Romans 8:32 CEV).

Do yourself a favor: Take your anxious moments to the cross. Leave them there with your bad moments, your mad moments, and your sad moments.

Sins. Faults. Troubles. Worries. Issues. Whatever we may call it, we *all* carry "baggage" of some kind or another. Things that weigh us down, drag at our spirits. And you know what? We don't have to! We don't have to carry any of it any longer than we *choose* to! Because Jesus is waiting to lift these burdens from us. And wipe them all away. All we have to do is ask. At the cross.

And may I suggest one more thing to take to the cross? Your *final moment*.

Barring the return of Christ first, you and I will have one. A final moment. A final breath. A final widening of the eyes and beating of the heart. In a split second you'll leave what you know and enter what you don't.

That's what bothers us. Death is the great unknown. We're always a bit skittish about the unknown.

My daughter Sara certainly was. My wife and I thought it was a great idea. We would kidnap the girls from school and take them on a weekend trip. We made reservations at a hotel and cleared the trip with their teachers, but kept it a secret from our girls. When we showed up at Sara's fourth-grade classroom on Friday afternoon, we thought she'd be thrilled. She wasn't. She was afraid. She didn't want to leave!

As we left, I assured her nothing was wrong. We had come to take her to a fun place. Didn't work. By the time we got to the car, she was crying. She was confused. She didn't like the interruption.

Nor do we. God promises to come at an unexpected hour and take us from the gray world we know to a golden world we don't. But since we don't, we aren't sure we want to go. We even get upset at the thought of his coming.

For that reason God wants us to do what Sara finally did—trust her father. "Don't let your hearts be troubled," he urged. "I will come back and take you to be with me so that you may be where I am" (John 14:1, 3).

By the way, in a short time Sara relaxed and enjoyed the trip. In fact, she didn't want to come back. You won't want to, either.

Troubled about your final moments? Leave them at the foot of the cross.

Leave them there with your bad moments, mad moments, anxious moments, and sad moments.

About this time someone is thinking, *You know, if I leave all those moments at the cross, I won't have any moments left but good ones.*

Well, what do you know? I guess you won't.